STO

GRAPHIC LIBRARY ™

GRAPHIC BIOGRAPHIES

Theodore Roosevelt

❖ BEAR OF A PRESIDENT ❖

by Nathan Olson

illustrated by Cynthia Martin,

Mark G. Heike, and

Barbara Schulz

Consultant:
Charles Markis
Chief of Interpretation and Visitors' Services
Sagamore Hill National Historic Site
Oyster Bay, New York

Capstone press ®

Mankato, Minnesota

Graphic Library is published by Capstone Press,
151 Good Counsel Drive, P.O. Box 669, Mankato, Minnesota 56002.
www.capstonepress.com

Printed in the United States of America

1 2 3 4 5 6 12 11 10 09 08 07

Library of Congress Cataloging-in-Publication Data
Olson, Nathan.
Theodore Roosevelt: bear of a president / by Nathan Olson; illustrated by Cynthia Martin, Mark Heike, and Barbara Schulz.
p. cm.—(Graphic library. Graphic biographies)
Includes bibliographical references and index.
ISBN-13: 978-0-7368-6849-5 (hardcover)
ISBN-10: 0-7368-6849-6 (hardcover)
ISBN-13: 978-0-7368-7901-9 (softcover pbk.)
ISBN-10: 0-7368-7901-3 (softcover pbk.)
1. Roosevelt, Theodore, 1858–1919—Juvenile literature. 2. Presidents—United States—Biography—Juvenile literature. 3. Graphic novels. I. Martin, Cynthia, 1961– ill. II. Heike, Mark, ill. III. Schulz, Barbara, ill. IV. Title. V. Series.
E757.O45 2005
973.91'1092—dc22 2006027984

Summary: In graphic novel format, tells the dramatic life story of President Theodore Roosevelt, whose strong will and leadership skills helped him pass many social, political, and conservation reforms.

Designers
Alison Thiele and Thomas Emery

Colorists
Cynthia Martin and Tami Collins

Production Designer
Kim Brown

Editor
Christine Peterson

Photo Credit
Corel, 1, 2–3, 28–29, 30–31, 32

Editor's note: Direct quotations from primary sources are indicated by a yellow background.

Direct quotations appear on the following pages:
Page 9, from *Theodore Roosevelt: An Autobiography* by Theodore Roosevelt (New York: The MacMillian Company, 1913).
Page 11, from a February 14, 1884, entry in Theodore Roosevelt's diary, part of the Theodore Roosevelt Papers Collection at the Library of Congress (http://lcweb2.loc.gov/ammem/trhtml/trhome.html).
Page 16, from a 1908 letter by Roosevelt; page 23 (top), from a 1912 speech by Roosevelt before the Progressive National Convention; page 23 (bottom), from Roosevelt's second annual message on December 2, 1902; as recorded at the Theodore Roosevelt Association (http://www.theodoreroosevelt.org/TR%20Web%20Book/Index.html).
Page 18, from a June 28, 1912, letter by Roosevelt, as published in *The Days of My Life, an Autobiography by Sir H. Rider Haggard* by H. Rider Haggard (London, New York: Longmans, Green, and Company, 1926).
Page 13, from a letter by Roosevelt; page 14, from a letter by Roosevelt; page 17, from a 1918 interview with Roosevelt; page 19, quote attributed to Republican Party leader Mark Hanna; as recorded in *T. R.: The Last Romantic* by H. W. Brands (New York: Basic Books, 1997).

Table of Contents

CHAPTER 1

Pain and Privilege

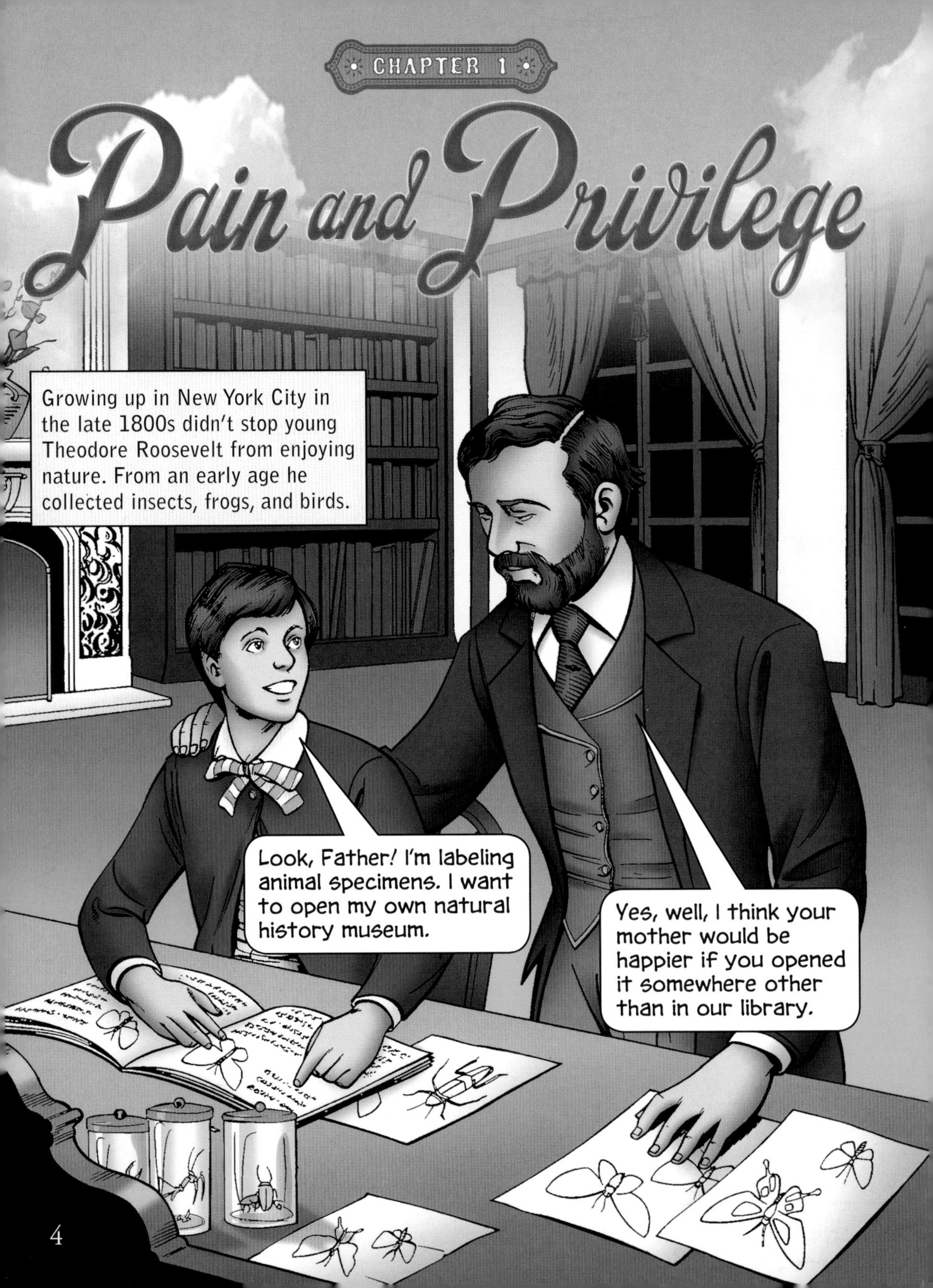
Growing up in New York City in the late 1800s didn't stop young Theodore Roosevelt from enjoying nature. From an early age he collected insects, frogs, and birds.
Look, Father! I'm labeling animal specimens. I want to open my own natural history museum.
Yes, well, I think your mother would be happier if you opened it somewhere other than in our library.

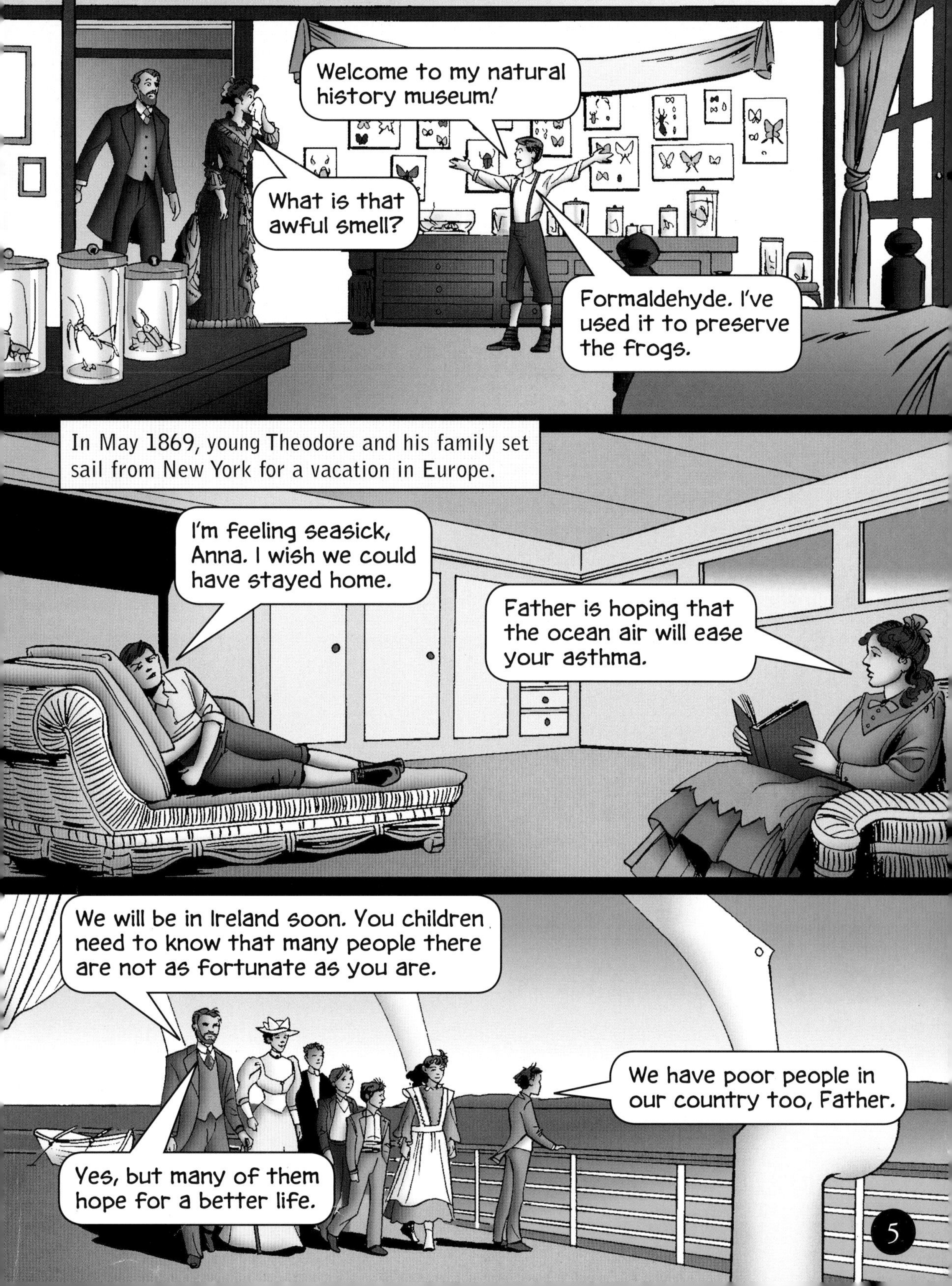
Welcome to my natural history museum!
What is that awful smell?
Formaldehyde. I've used it to preserve the frogs.
In May 1869, young Theodore and his family set sail from New York for a vacation in Europe.
I'm feeling seasick, Anna. I wish we could have stayed home.
Father is hoping that the ocean air will ease your asthma.
We will be in Ireland soon. You children need to know that many people there are not as fortunate as you are.
We have poor people in our country too, Father.
Yes, but many of them hope for a better life.

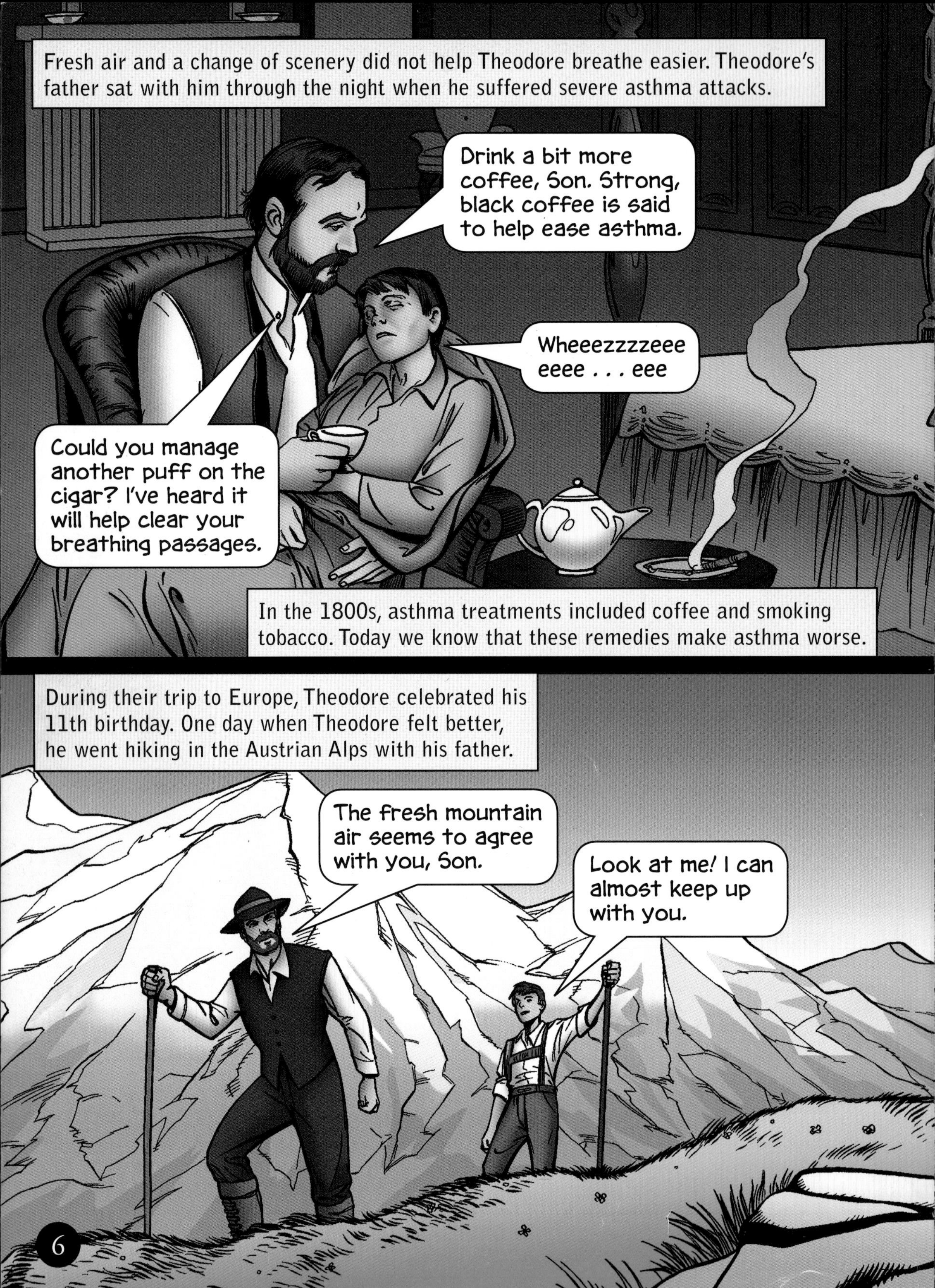
Fresh air and a change of scenery did not help Theodore breathe easier. Theodore's father sat with him through the night when he suffered severe asthma attacks.
Drink a bit more coffee, Son. Strong, black coffee is said to help ease asthma.
Wheeezzzzeee eeee . . . eee
Could you manage another puff on the cigar? I've heard it will help clear your breathing passages.
In the 1800s, asthma treatments included coffee and smoking tobacco. Today we know that these remedies make asthma worse.
During their trip to Europe, Theodore celebrated his 11th birthday. One day when Theodore felt better, he went hiking in the Austrian Alps with his father.
The fresh mountain air seems to agree with you, Son.
Look at me! I can almost keep up with you.

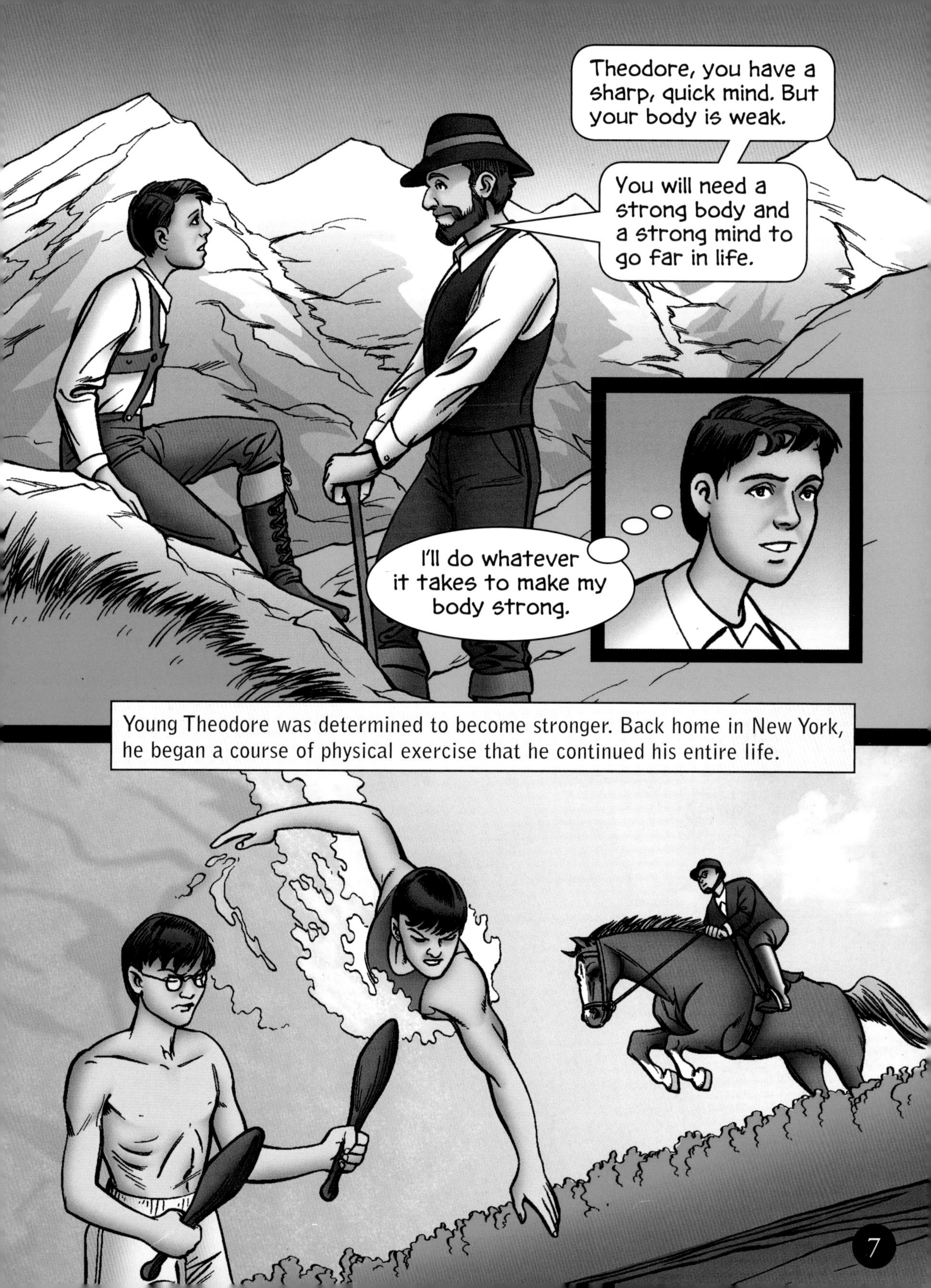
Theodore, you have a sharp, quick mind. But your body is weak.
You will need a strong body and a strong mind to go far in life.
I'll do whatever it takes to make my body strong.
Young Theodore was determined to become stronger. Back home in New York, he began a course of physical exercise that he continued his entire life.

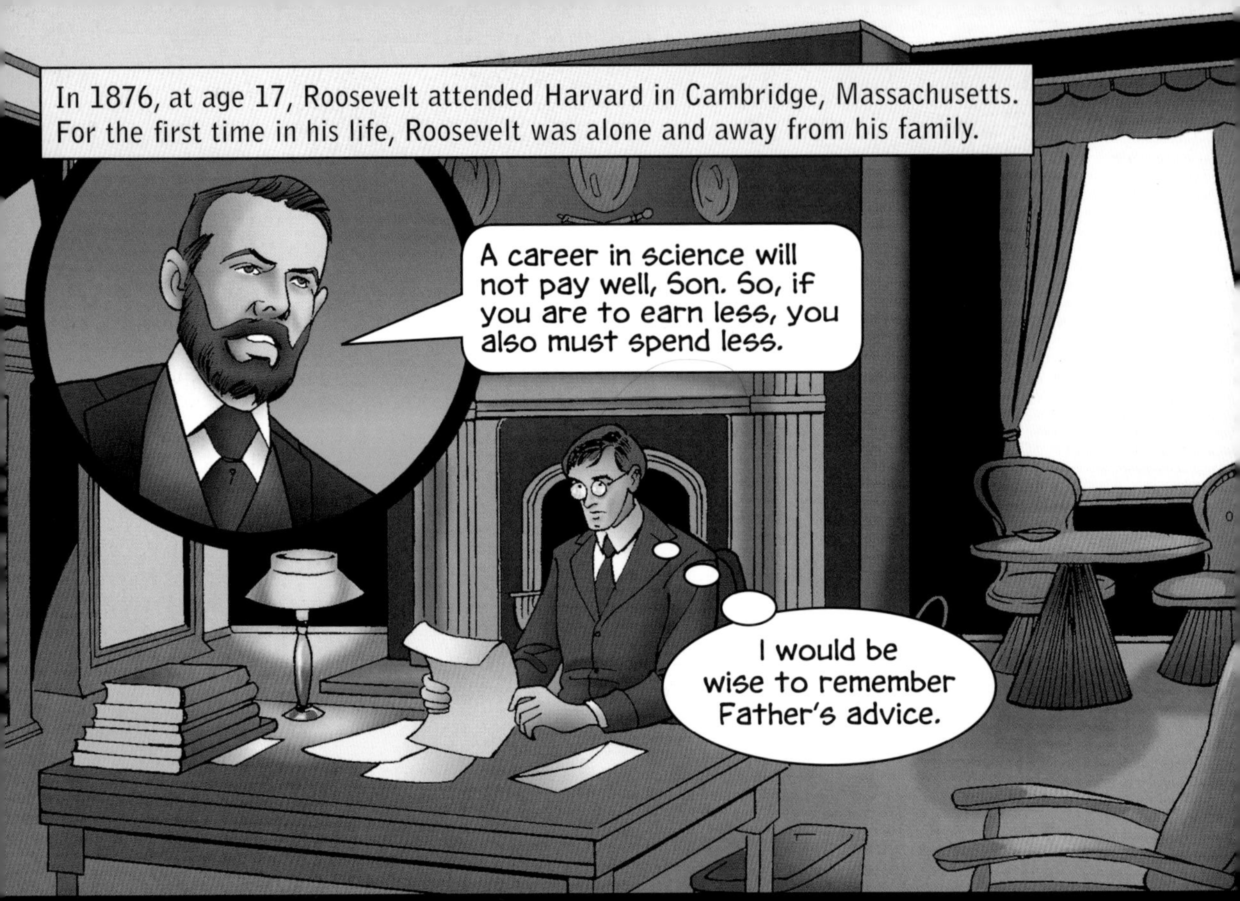
In 1876, at age 17, Roosevelt attended Harvard in Cambridge, Massachusetts. For the first time in his life, Roosevelt was alone and away from his family.
A career in science will not pay well, Son. So, if you are to earn less, you also must spend less.
I would be wise to remember Father's advice.

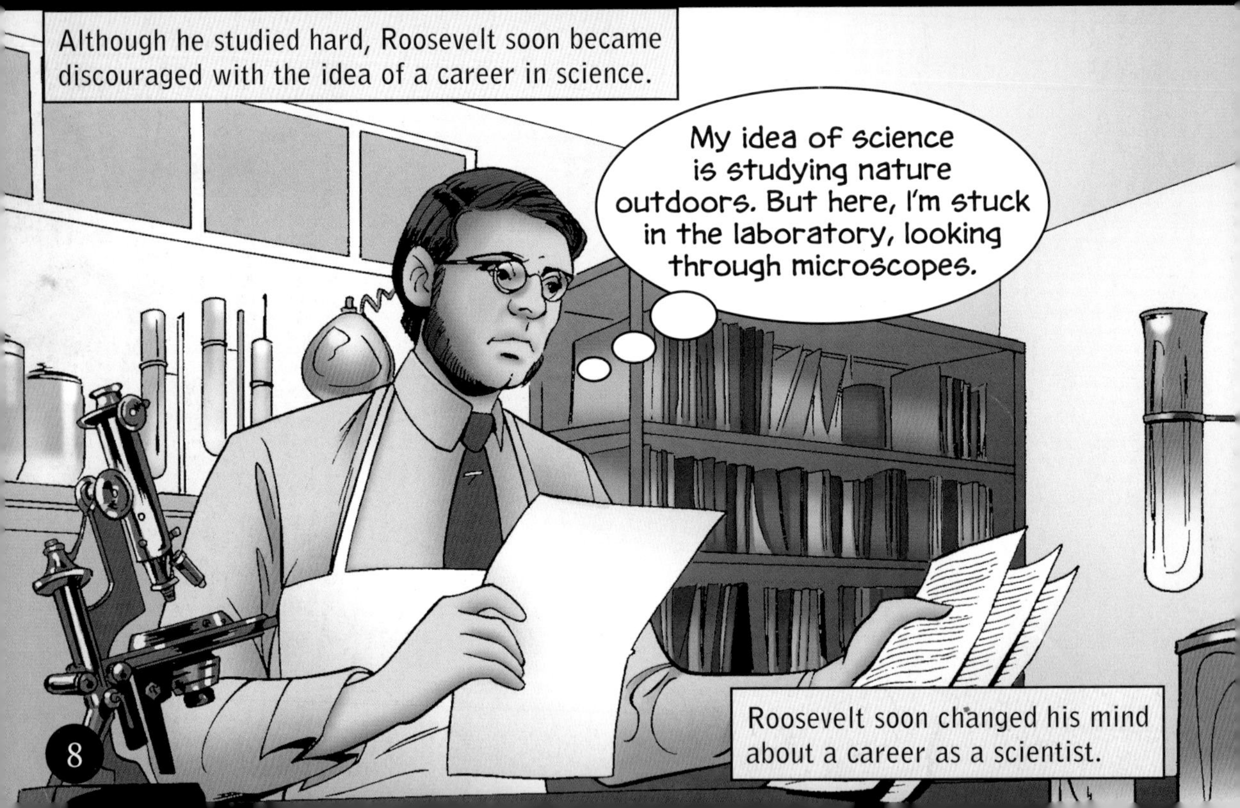
Although he studied hard, Roosevelt soon became discouraged with the idea of a career in science.
My idea of science is studying nature outdoors. But here, I'm stuck in the laboratory, looking through microscopes.
Roosevelt soon changed his mind about a career as a scientist.

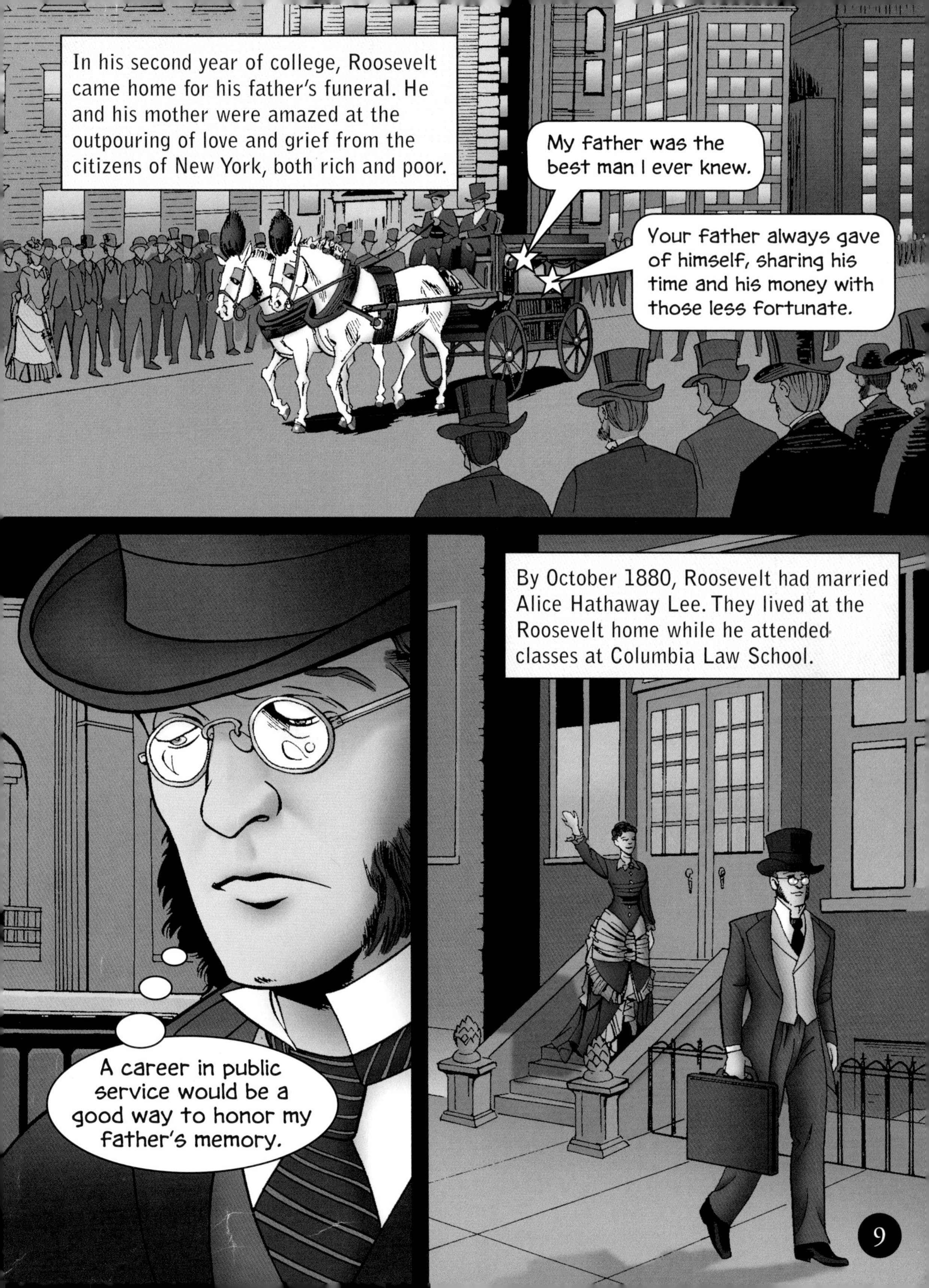
In his second year of college, Roosevelt came home for his father's funeral. He and his mother were amazed at the outpouring of love and grief from the citizens of New York, both rich and poor.
My father was the best man I ever knew.
Your father always gave of himself, sharing his time and his money with those less fortunate.
A career in public service would be a good way to honor my father's memory.
By October 1880, Roosevelt had married Alice Hathaway Lee. They lived at the Roosevelt home while he attended classes at Columbia Law School.

CHAPTER 2

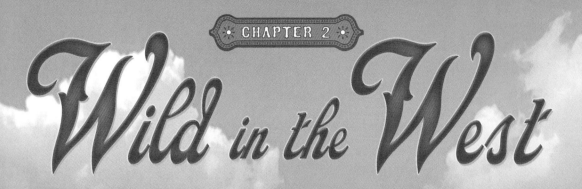

Wild in the West

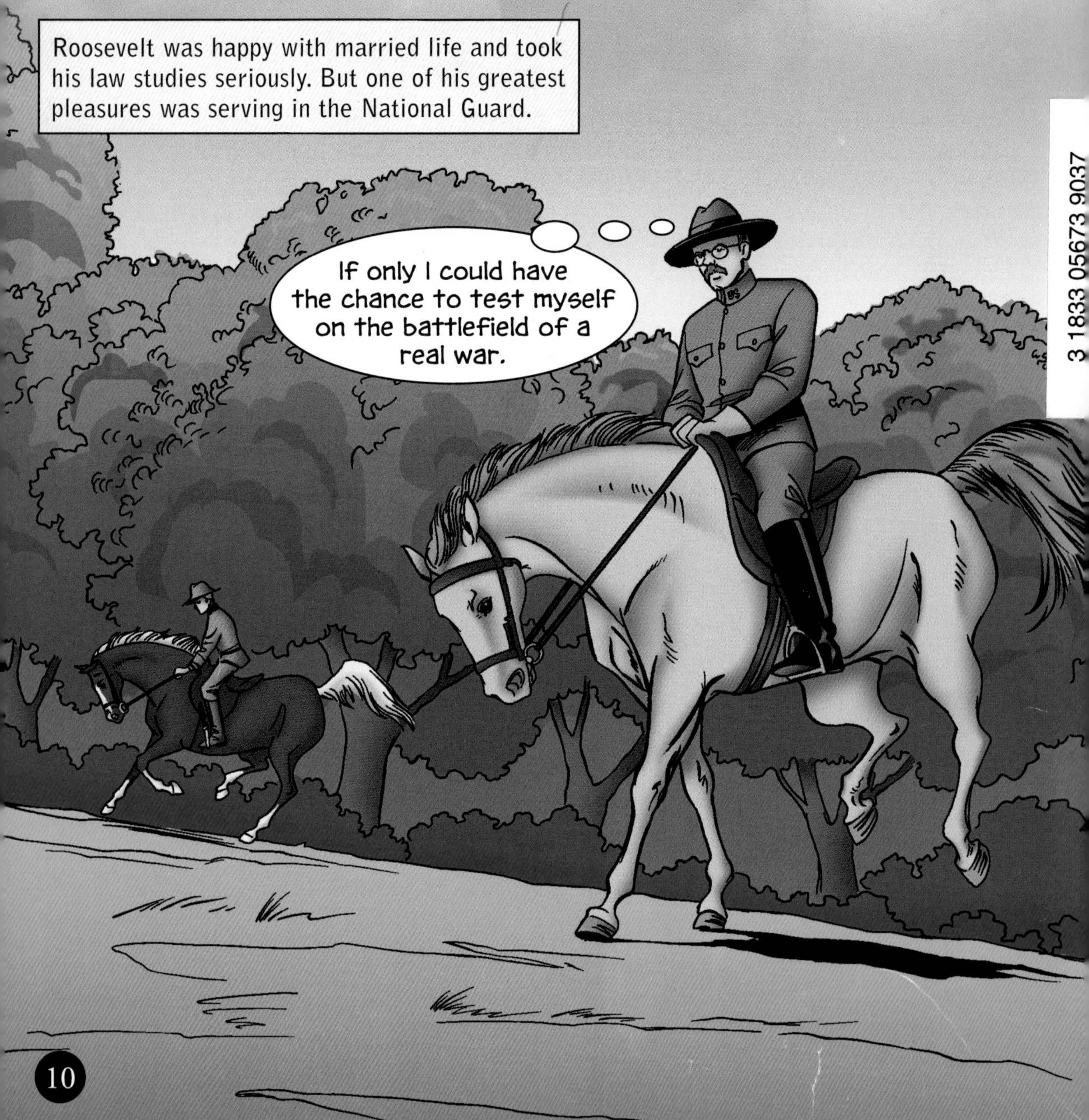
Roosevelt was happy with married life and took his law studies seriously. But one of his greatest pleasures was serving in the National Guard.
If only I could have the chance to test myself on the battlefield of a real war.

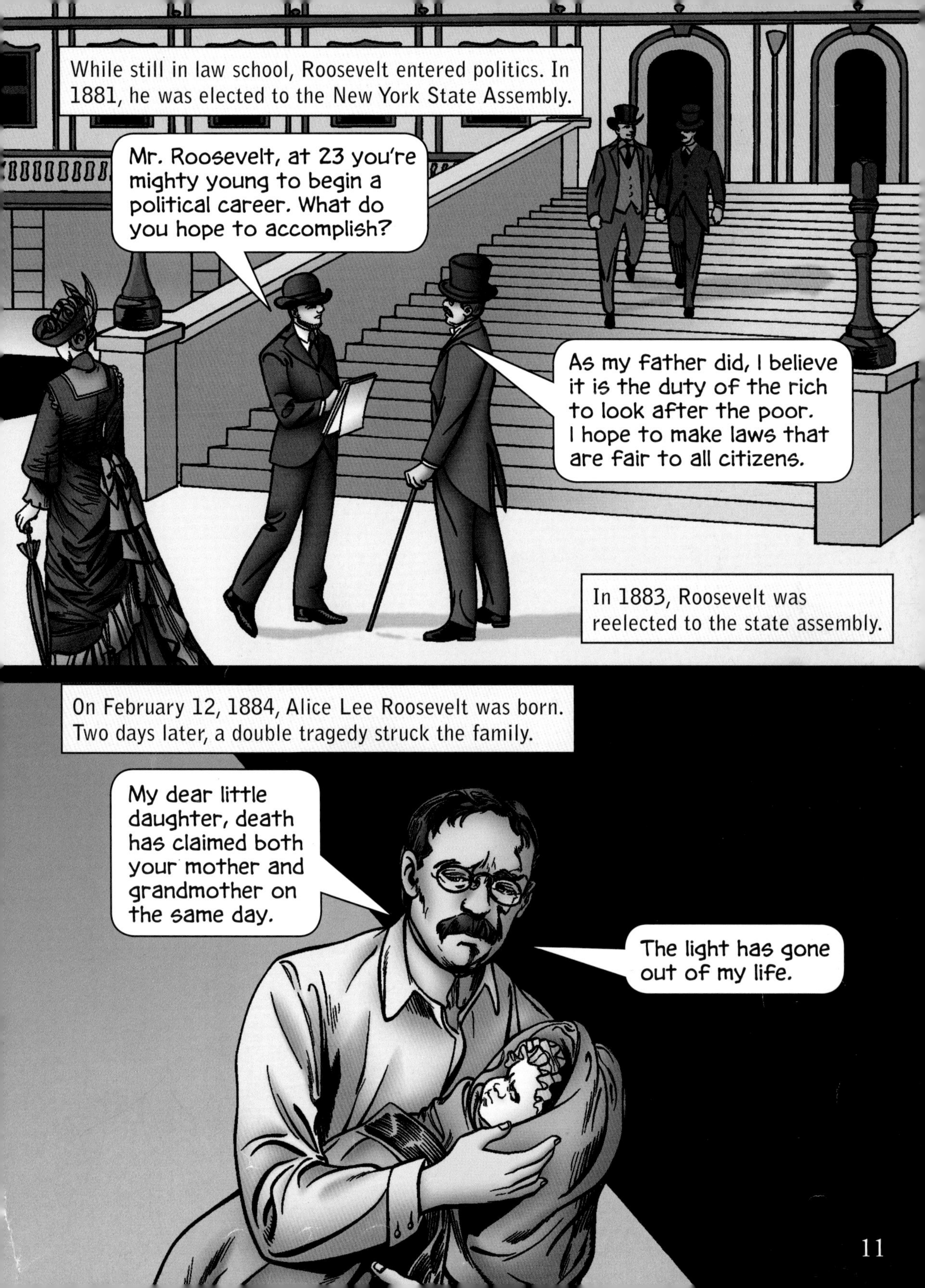
While still in law school, Roosevelt entered politics. In 1881, he was elected to the New York State Assembly.
Mr. Roosevelt, at 23 you're mighty young to begin a political career. What do you hope to accomplish?
As my father did, I believe it is the duty of the rich to look after the poor. I hope to make laws that are fair to all citizens.
In 1883, Roosevelt was reelected to the state assembly.
On February 12, 1884, Alice Lee Roosevelt was born. Two days later, a double tragedy struck the family.
My dear little daughter, death has claimed both your mother and grandmother on the same day.
The light has gone out of my life.

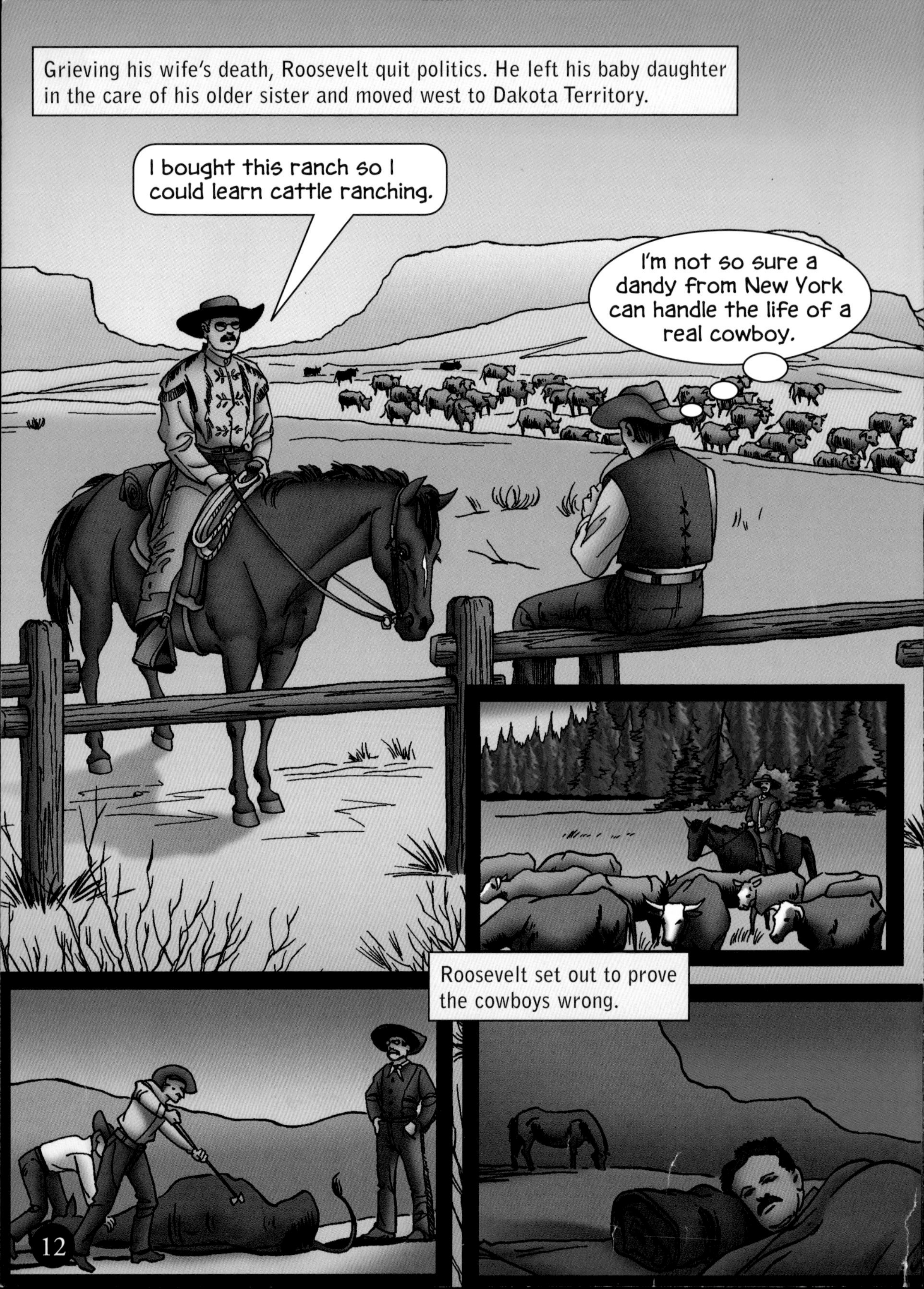
Grieving his wife's death, Roosevelt quit politics. He left his baby daughter in the care of his older sister and moved west to Dakota Territory.
I bought this ranch so I could learn cattle ranching.
I'm not so sure a dandy from New York can handle the life of a real cowboy.
Roosevelt set out to prove the cowboys wrong.

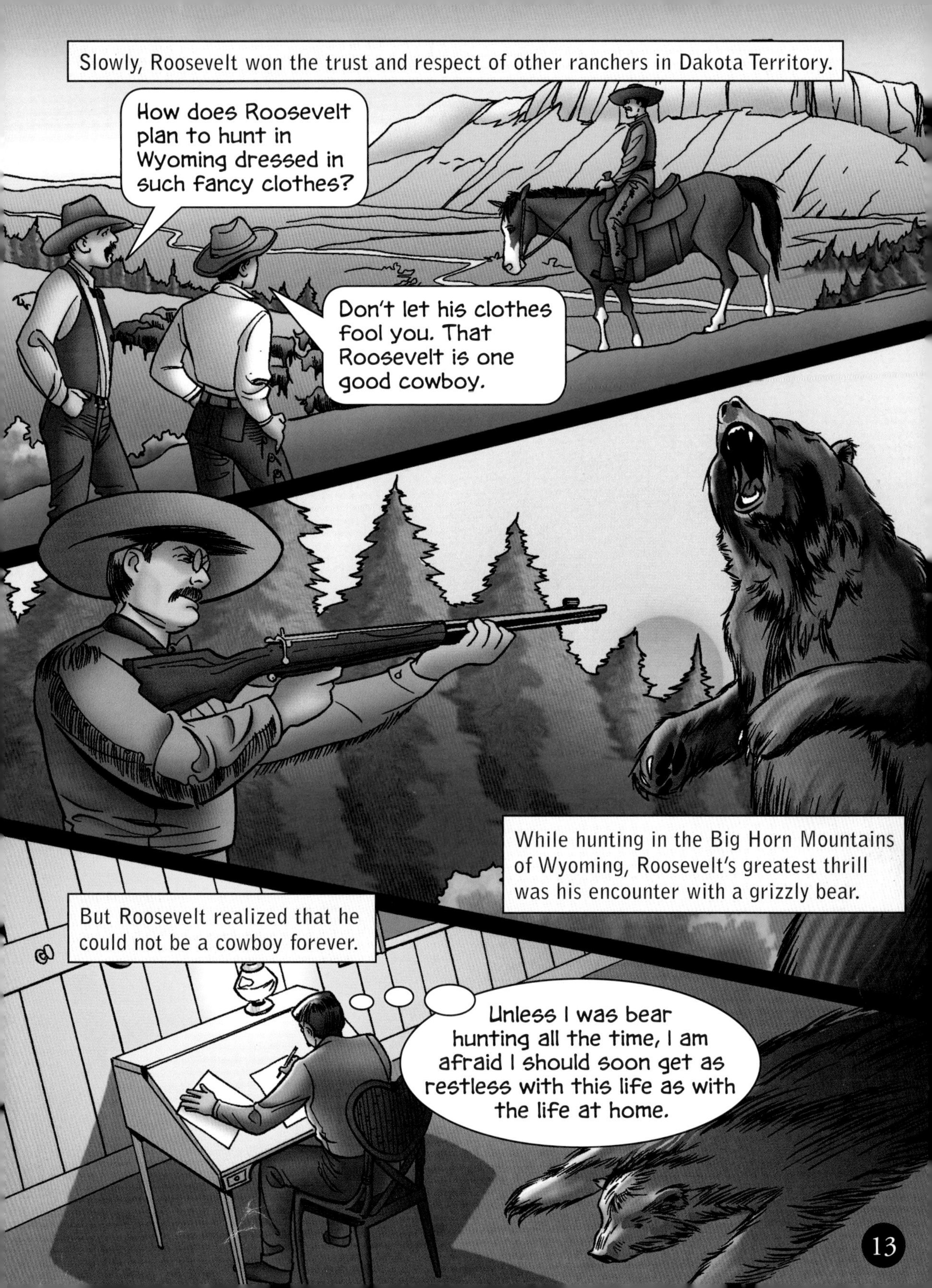
Slowly, Roosevelt won the trust and respect of other ranchers in Dakota Territory.
How does Roosevelt plan to hunt in Wyoming dressed in such fancy clothes?
Don't let his clothes fool you. That Roosevelt is one good cowboy.
While hunting in the Big Horn Mountains of Wyoming, Roosevelt's greatest thrill was his encounter with a grizzly bear.
But Roosevelt realized that he could not be a cowboy forever.
Unless I was bear hunting all the time, I am afraid I should soon get as restless with this life as with the life at home.

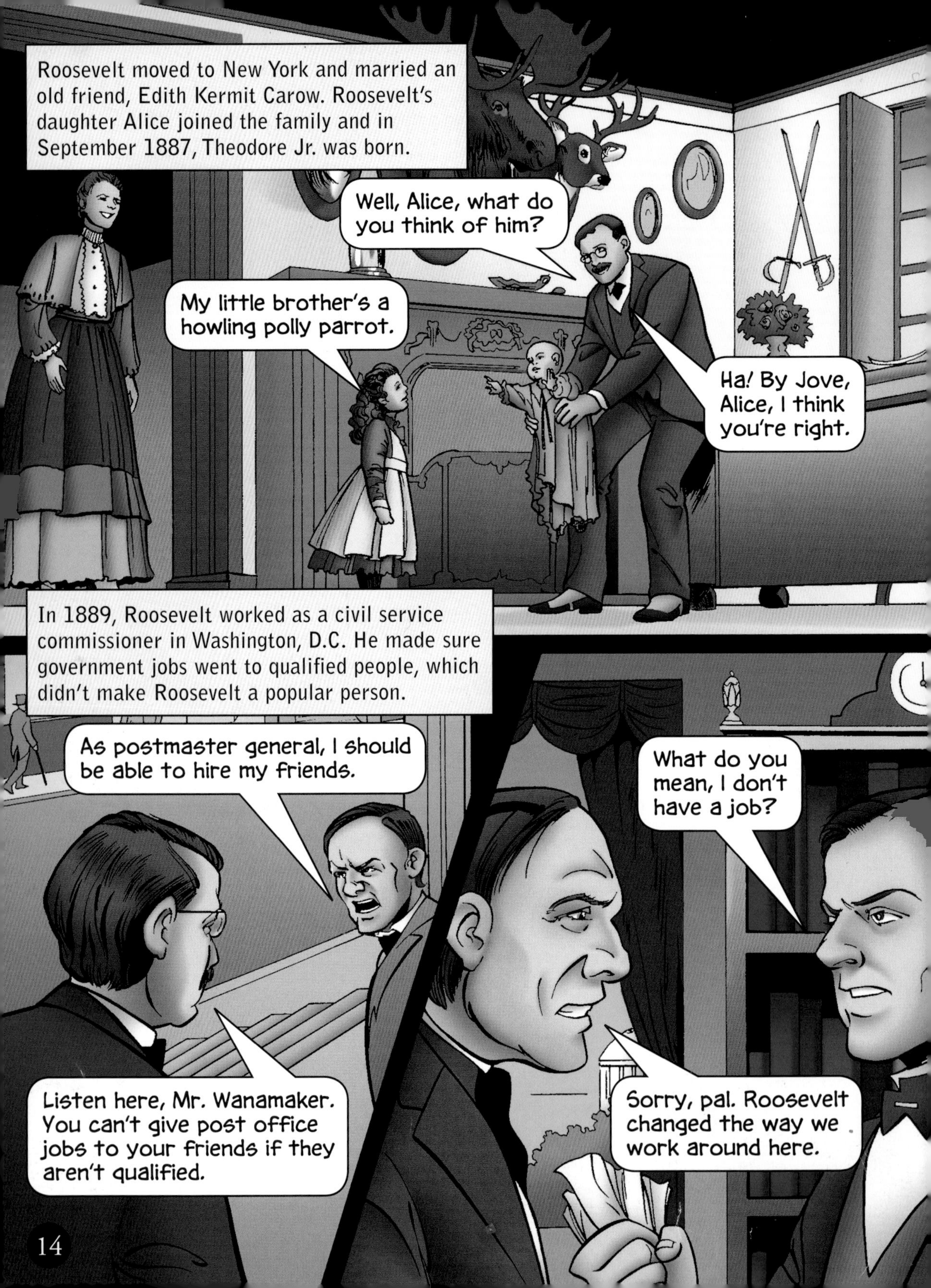
Roosevelt moved to New York and married an old friend, Edith Kermit Carow. Roosevelt's daughter Alice joined the family and in September 1887, Theodore Jr. was born.
Well, Alice, what do you think of him?
My little brother's a howling polly parrot.
Ha! By Jove, Alice, I think you're right.
In 1889, Roosevelt worked as a civil service commissioner in Washington, D.C. He made sure government jobs went to qualified people, which didn't make Roosevelt a popular person.
As postmaster general, I should be able to hire my friends.
Listen here, Mr. Wanamaker. You can't give post office jobs to your friends if they aren't qualified.
What do you mean, I don't have a job?
Sorry, pal. Roosevelt changed the way we work around here.

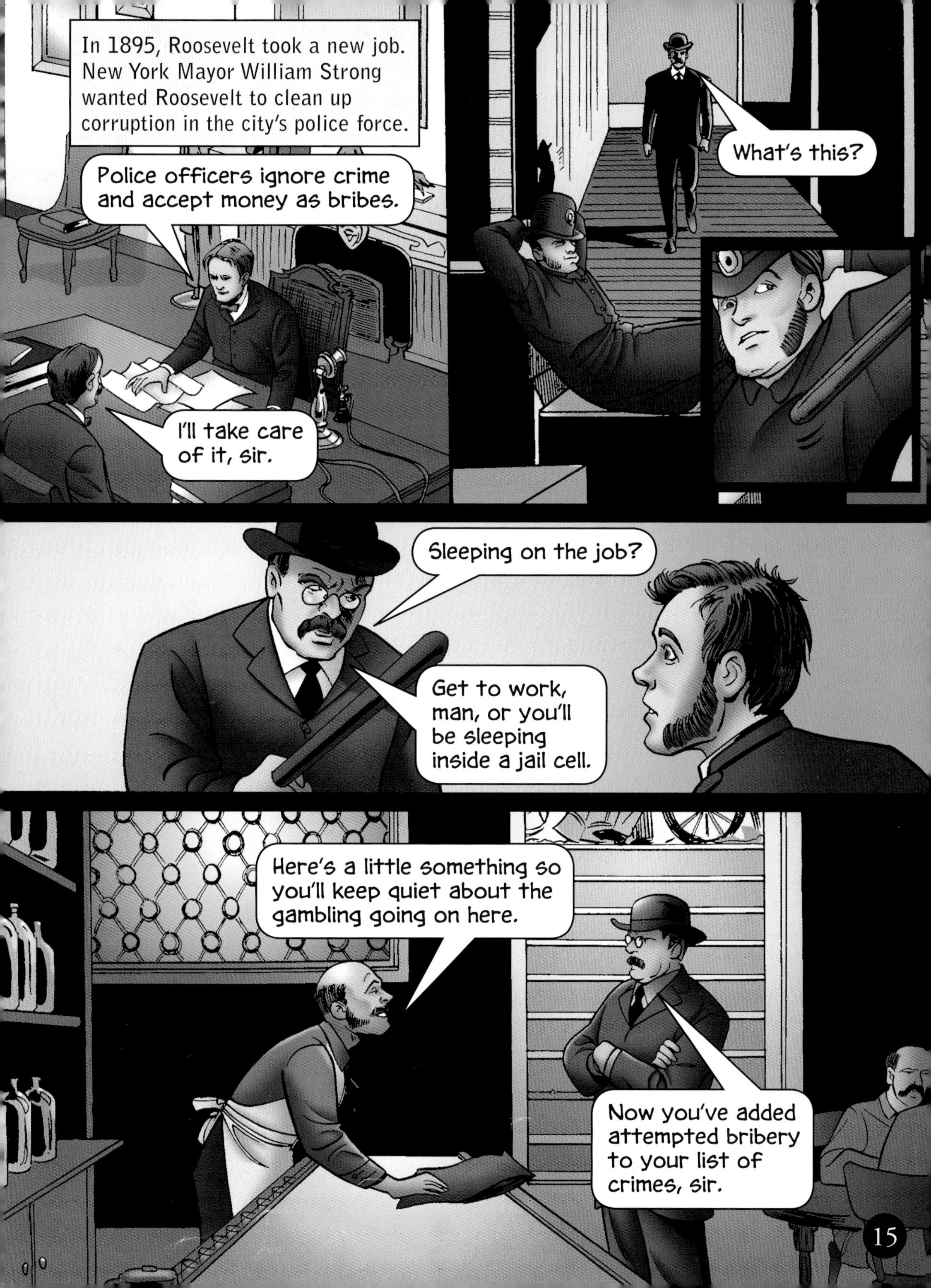

In 1895, Roosevelt took a new job. New York Mayor William Strong wanted Roosevelt to clean up corruption in the city's police force.
Police officers ignore crime and accept money as bribes.
I'll take care of it, sir.
What's this?
Sleeping on the job?
Get to work, man, or you'll be sleeping inside a jail cell.
Here's a little something so you'll keep quiet about the gambling going on here.
Now you've added attempted bribery to your list of crimes, sir.

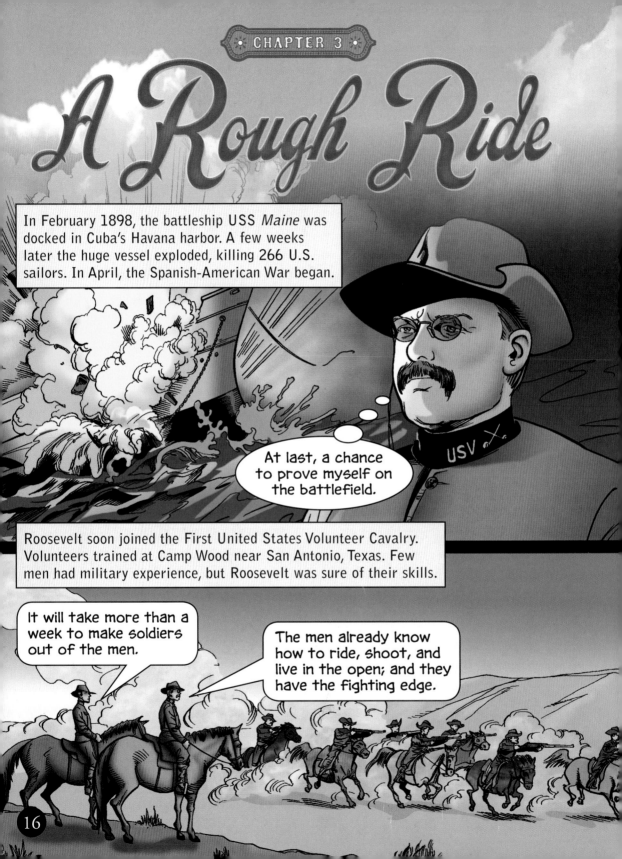

CHAPTER 3

A Rough Ride

In February 1898, the battleship USS *Maine* was docked in Cuba's Havana harbor. A few weeks later the huge vessel exploded, killing 266 U.S. sailors. In April, the Spanish-American War began.

At last, a chance to prove myself on the battlefield.

Roosevelt soon joined the First United States Volunteer Cavalry. Volunteers trained at Camp Wood near San Antonio, Texas. Few men had military experience, but Roosevelt was sure of their skills.

It will take more than a week to make soldiers out of the men.

The men already know how to ride, shoot, and live in the open; and they have the fighting edge.

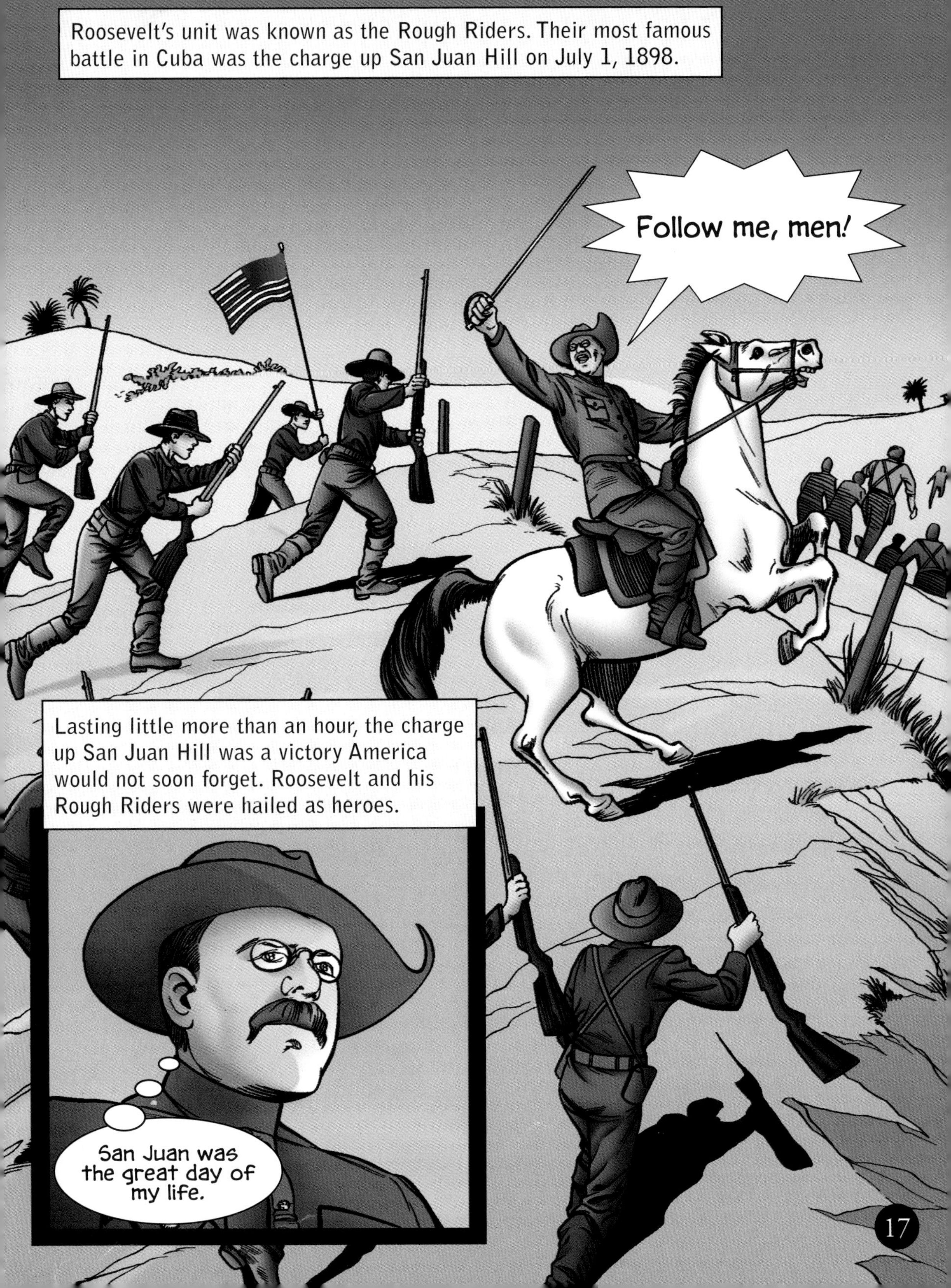
Roosevelt's unit was known as the Rough Riders. Their most famous battle in Cuba was the charge up San Juan Hill on July 1, 1898.
Follow me, men!
Lasting little more than an hour, the charge up San Juan Hill was a victory America would not soon forget. Roosevelt and his Rough Riders were hailed as heroes.
San Juan was the great day of my life.

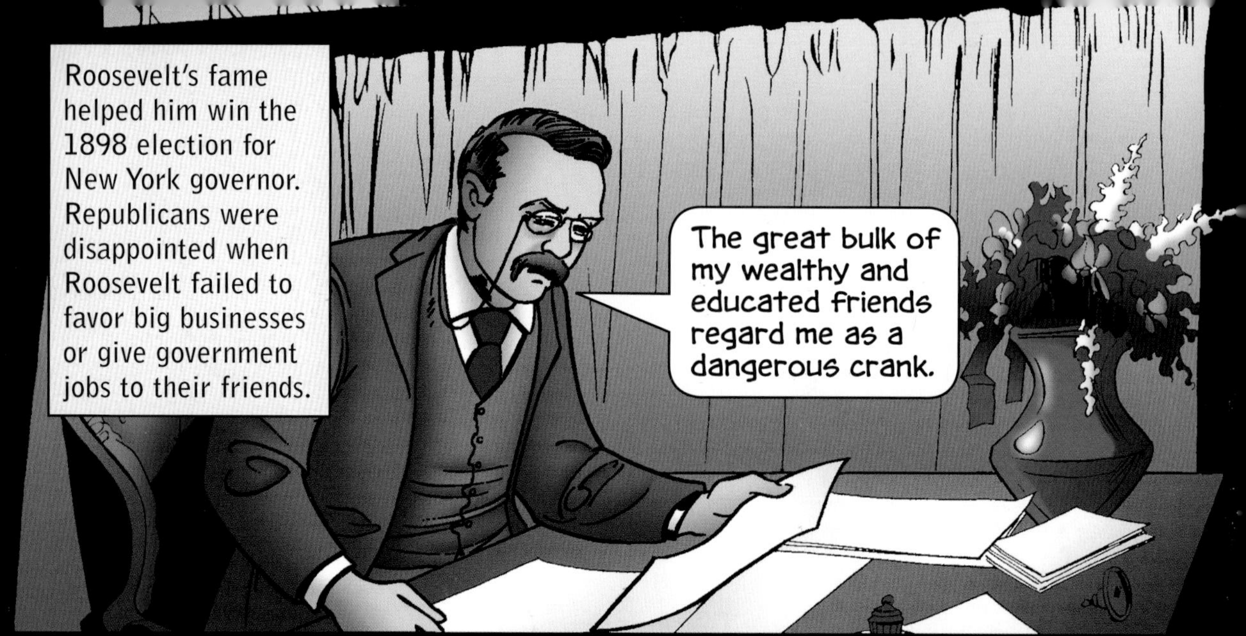
Roosevelt's fame helped him win the 1898 election for New York governor. Republicans were disappointed when Roosevelt failed to favor big businesses or give government jobs to their friends.
The great bulk of my wealthy and educated friends regard me as a dangerous crank.

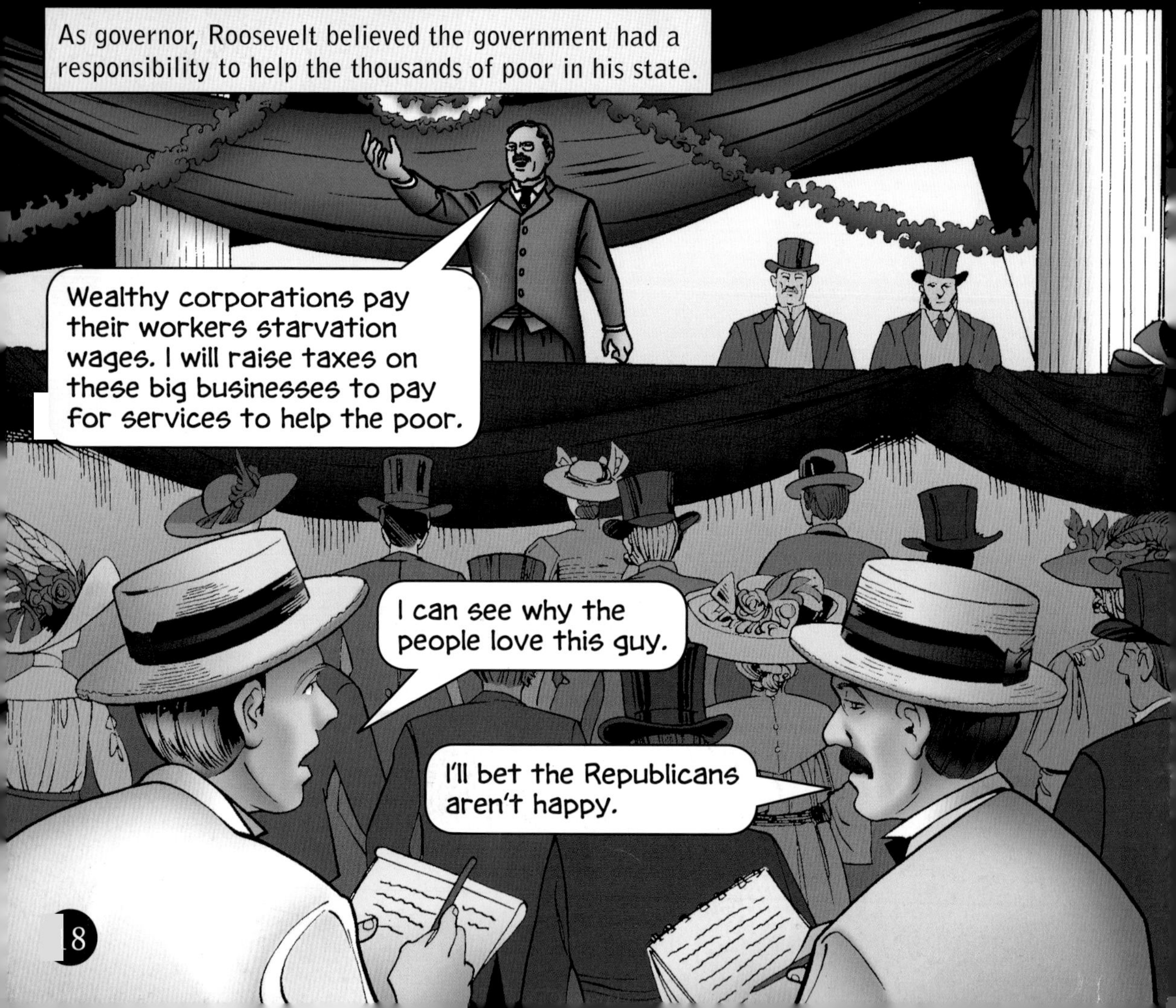
As governor, Roosevelt believed the government had a responsibility to help the thousands of poor in his state.
Wealthy corporations pay their workers starvation wages. I will raise taxes on these big businesses to pay for services to help the poor.
I can see why the people love this guy.
I'll bet the Republicans aren't happy.

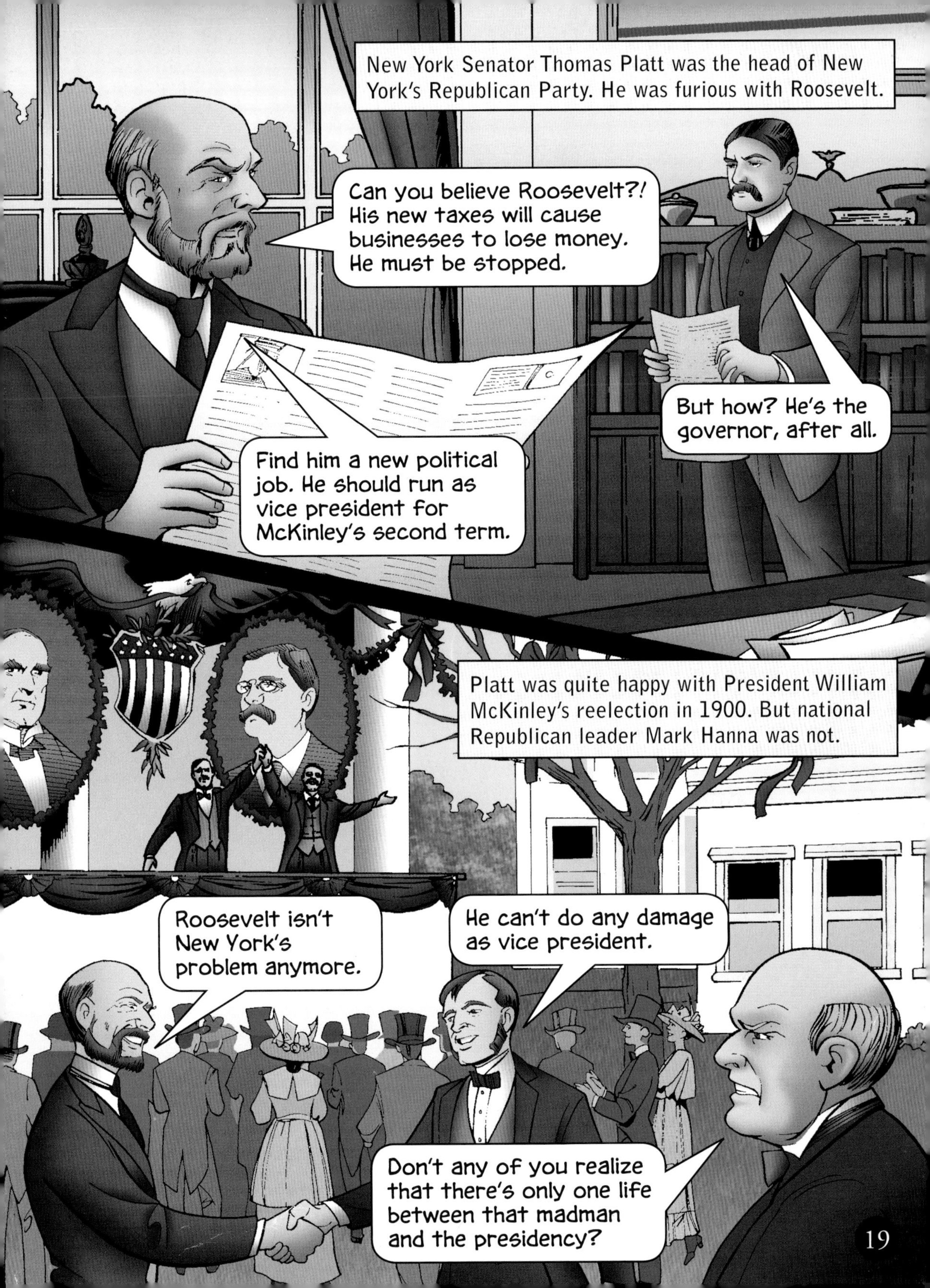

New York Senator Thomas Platt was the head of New York's Republican Party. He was furious with Roosevelt.
Can you believe Roosevelt?! His new taxes will cause businesses to lose money. He must be stopped.
But how? He's the governor, after all.
Find him a new political job. He should run as vice president for McKinley's second term.
Platt was quite happy with President William McKinley's reelection in 1900. But national Republican leader Mark Hanna was not.
Roosevelt isn't New York's problem anymore.
He can't do any damage as vice president.
Don't any of you realize that there's only one life between that madman and the presidency?

CHAPTER 4

Bear of a President

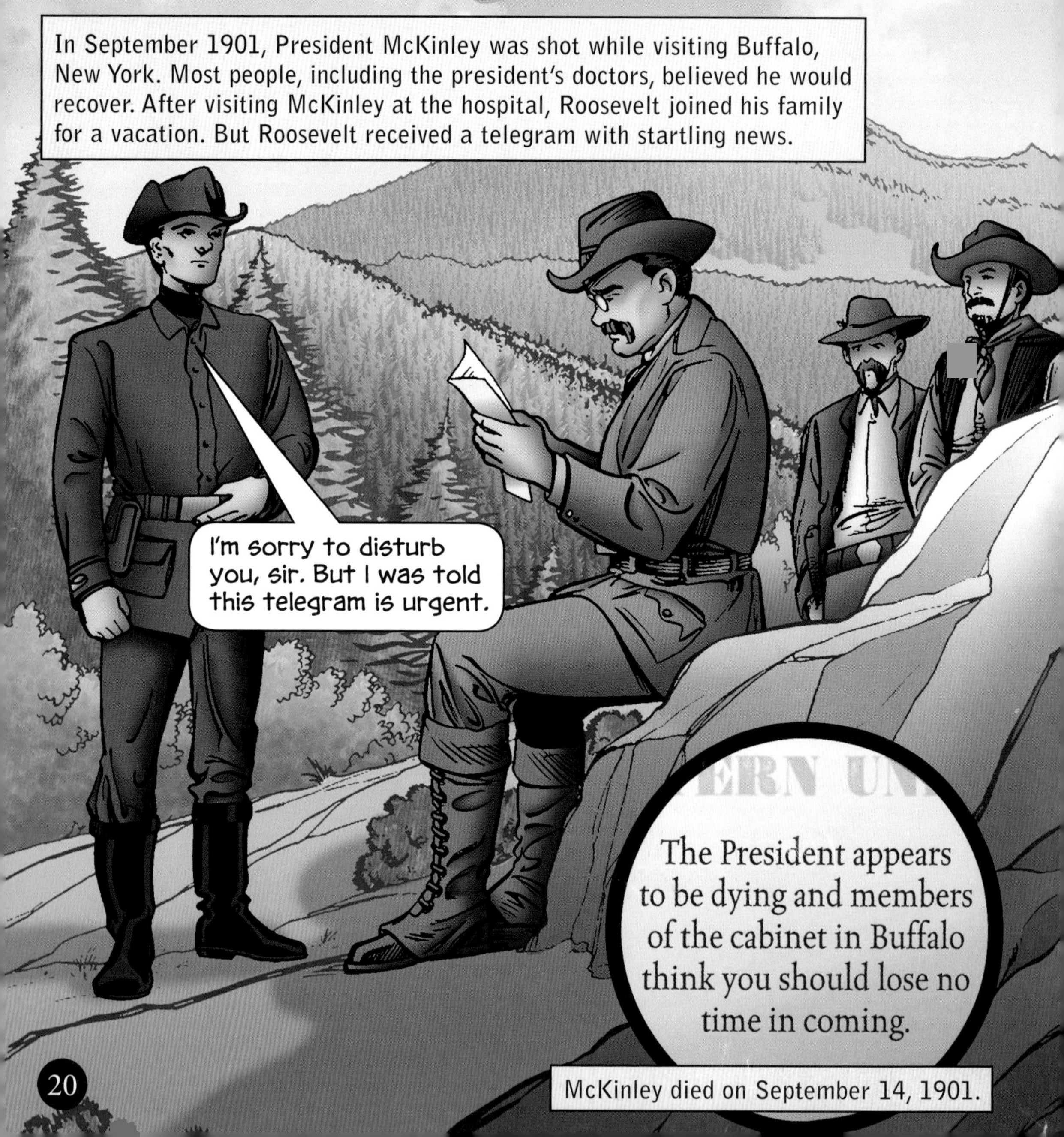
In September 1901, President McKinley was shot while visiting Buffalo, New York. Most people, including the president's doctors, believed he would recover. After visiting McKinley at the hospital, Roosevelt joined his family for a vacation. But Roosevelt received a telegram with startling news.
I'm sorry to disturb you, sir. But I was told this telegram is urgent.
The President appears to be dying and members of the cabinet in Buffalo think you should lose no time in coming.
McKinley died on September 14, 1901.

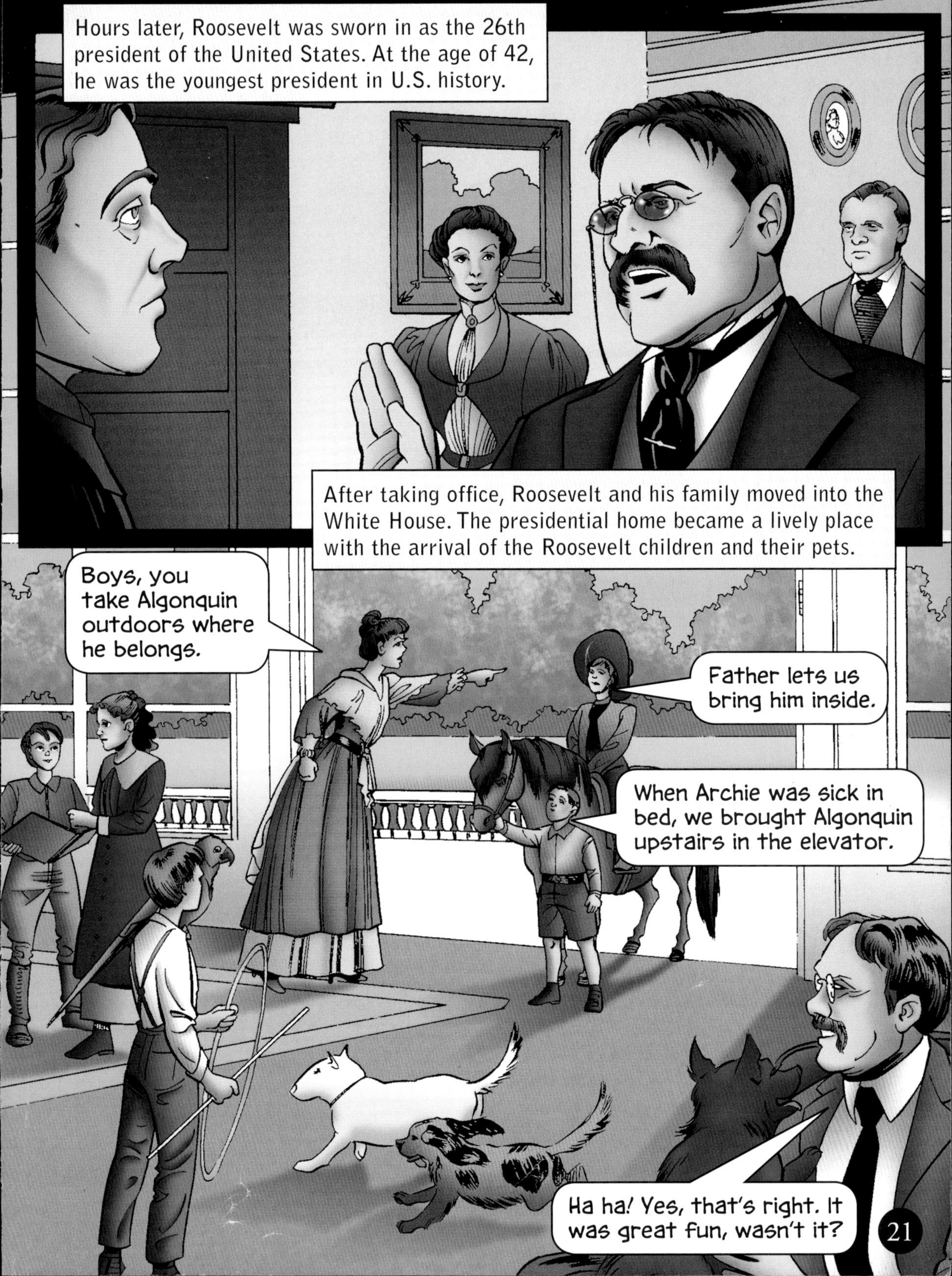
Hours later, Roosevelt was sworn in as the 26th president of the United States. At the age of 42, he was the youngest president in U.S. history.
After taking office, Roosevelt and his family moved into the White House. The presidential home became a lively place with the arrival of the Roosevelt children and their pets.
Boys, you take Algonquin outdoors where he belongs.
Father lets us bring him inside.
When Archie was sick in bed, we brought Algonquin upstairs in the elevator.
Ha ha! Yes, that's right. It was great fun, wasn't it?

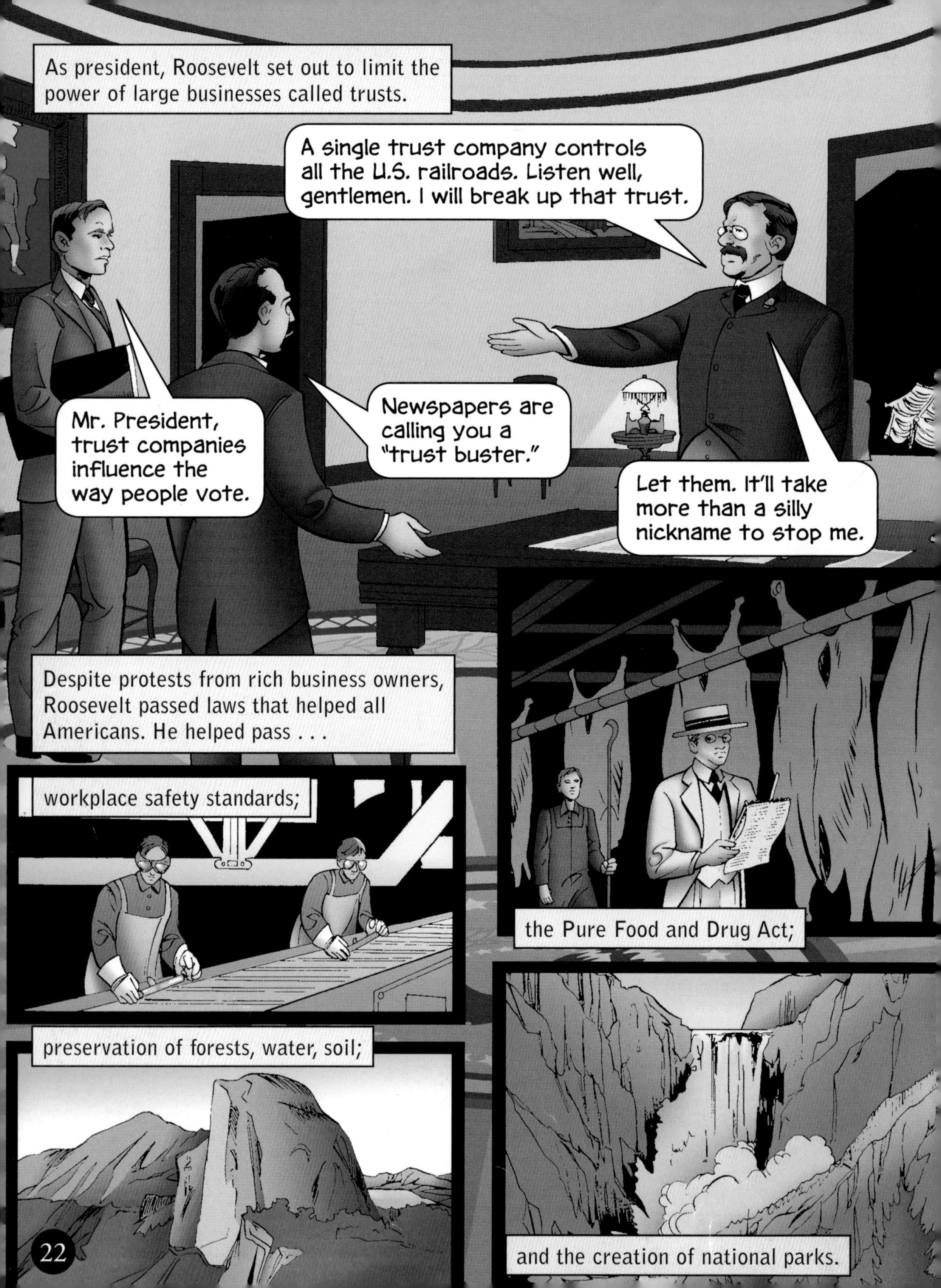

As president, Roosevelt set out to limit the power of large businesses called trusts.
A single trust company controls all the U.S. railroads. Listen well, gentlemen. I will break up that trust.
Mr. President, trust companies influence the way people vote.
Newspapers are calling you a "trust buster."
Let them. It'll take more than a silly nickname to stop me.
Despite protests from rich business owners, Roosevelt passed laws that helped all Americans. He helped pass . . .
workplace safety standards;
the Pure Food and Drug Act;
preservation of forests, water, soil;
and the creation of national parks.

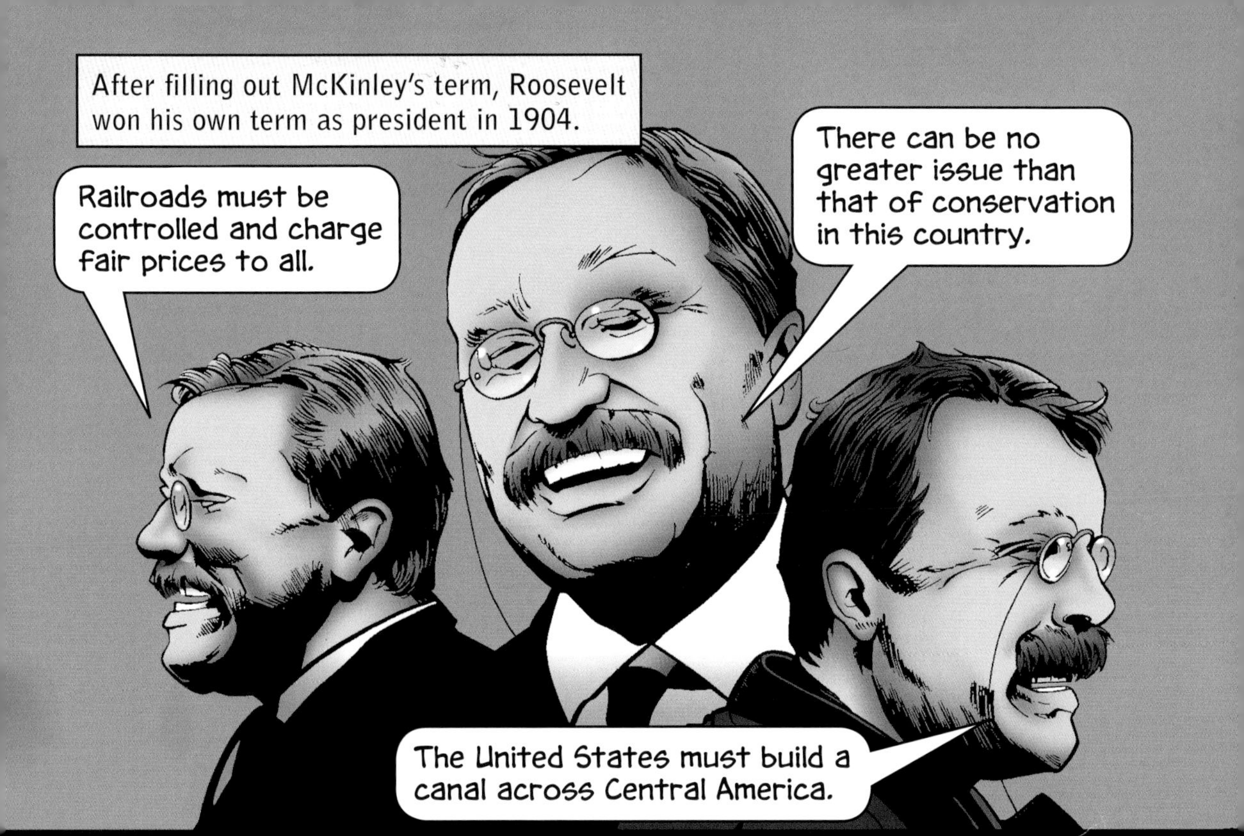
After filling out McKinley's term, Roosevelt won his own term as president in 1904.
Railroads must be controlled and charge fair prices to all.
There can be no greater issue than that of conservation in this country.
The United States must build a canal across Central America.

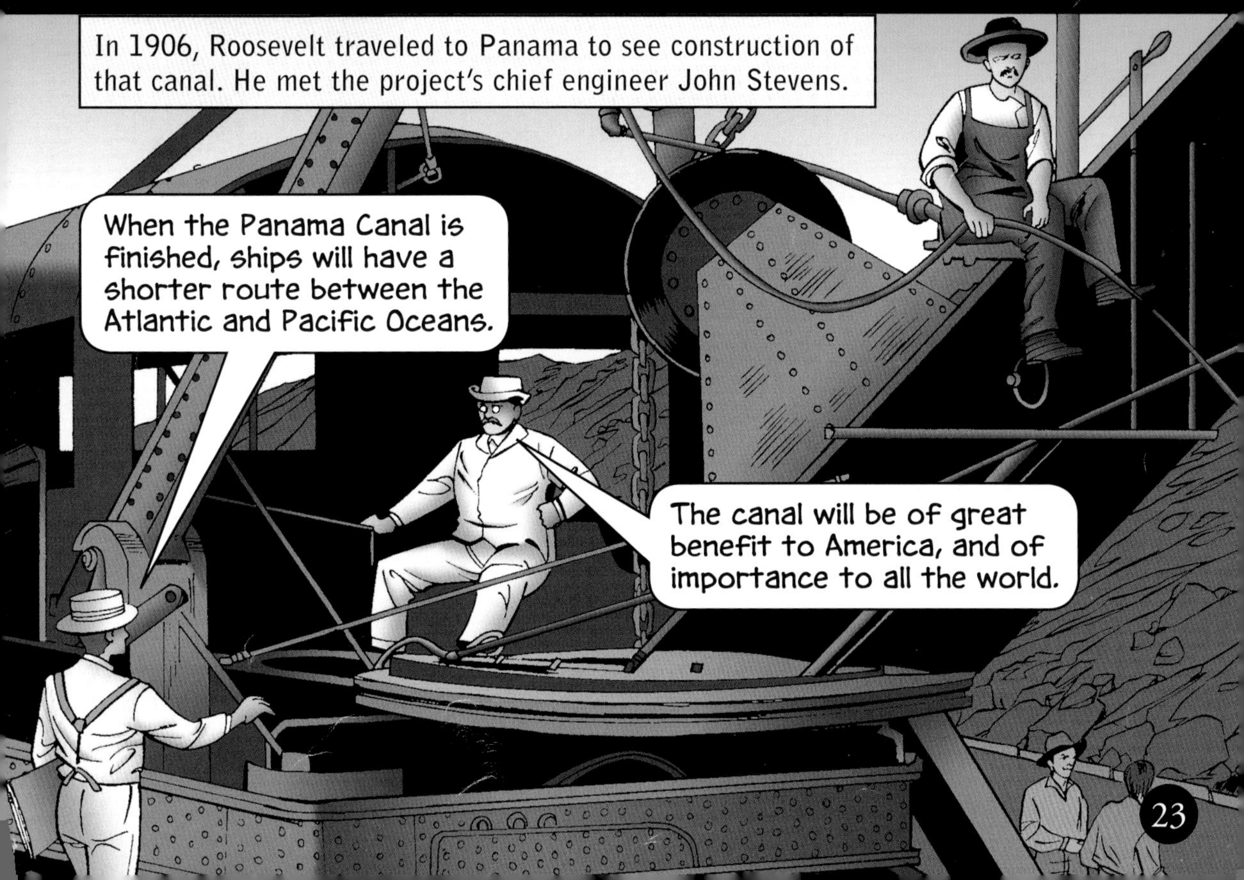
In 1906, Roosevelt traveled to Panama to see construction of that canal. He met the project's chief engineer John Stevens.
When the Panama Canal is finished, ships will have a shorter route between the Atlantic and Pacific Oceans.
The canal will be of great benefit to America, and of importance to all the world.

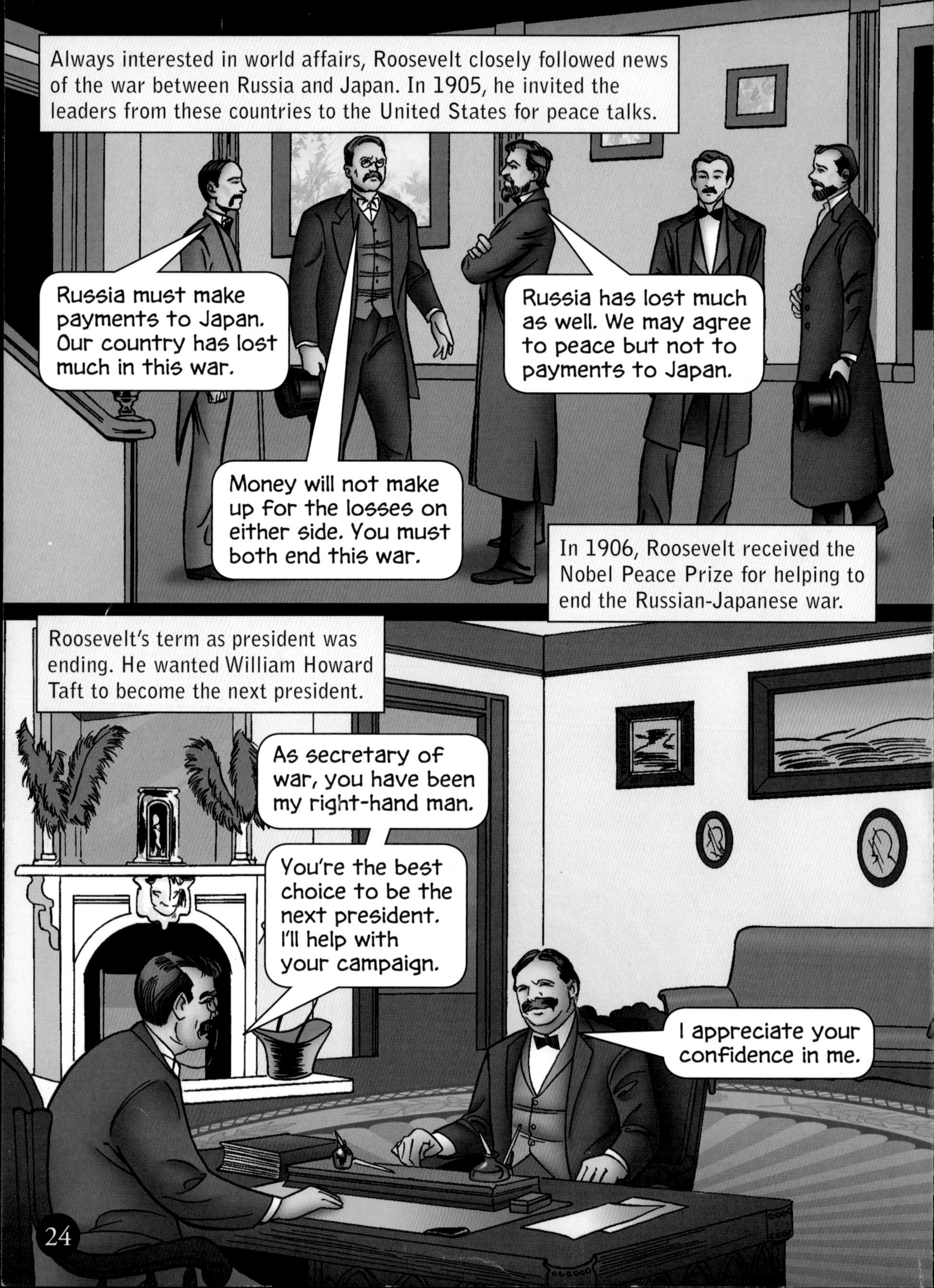
Always interested in world affairs, Roosevelt closely followed news of the war between Russia and Japan. In 1905, he invited the leaders from these countries to the United States for peace talks.
Russia must make payments to Japan. Our country has lost much in this war.
Money will not make up for the losses on either side. You must both end this war.
Russia has lost much as well. We may agree to peace but not to payments to Japan.
In 1906, Roosevelt received the Nobel Peace Prize for helping to end the Russian-Japanese war.
Roosevelt's term as president was ending. He wanted William Howard Taft to become the next president.
As secretary of war, you have been my right-hand man.
You're the best choice to be the next president. I'll help with your campaign.
I appreciate your confidence in me.

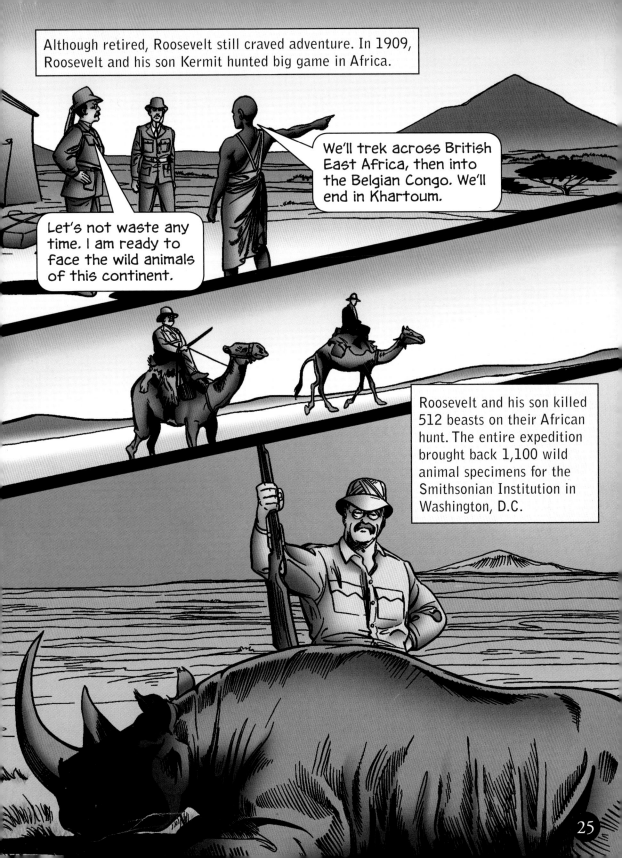

Although retired, Roosevelt still craved adventure. In 1909, Roosevelt and his son Kermit hunted big game in Africa.

We'll trek across British East Africa, then into the Belgian Congo. We'll end in Khartoum.

Let's not waste any time. I am ready to face the wild animals of this continent.

Roosevelt and his son killed 512 beasts on their African hunt. The entire expedition brought back 1,100 wild animal specimens for the Smithsonian Institution in Washington, D.C.

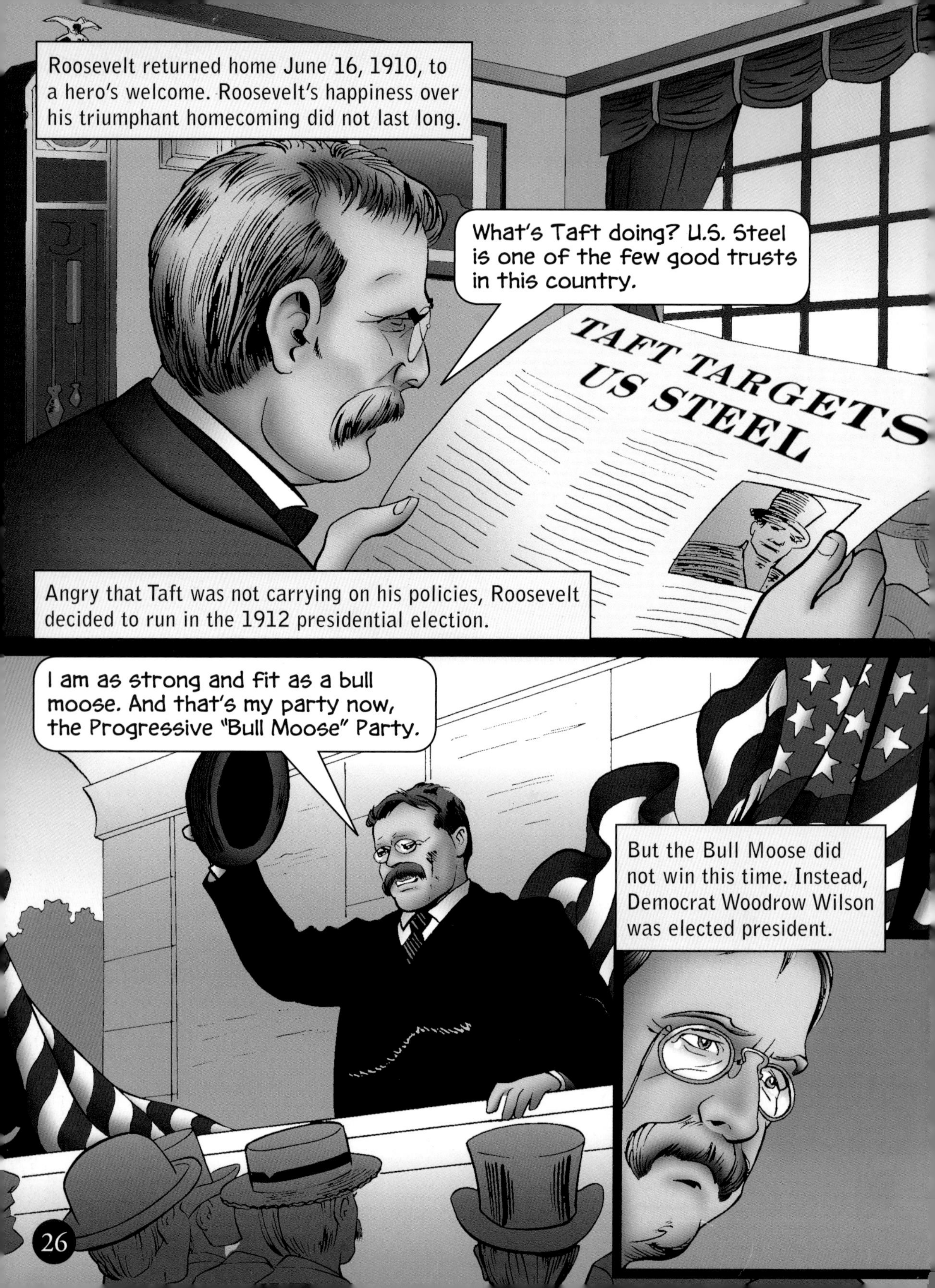

Roosevelt returned home June 16, 1910, to a hero's welcome. Roosevelt's happiness over his triumphant homecoming did not last long.
What's Taft doing? U.S. Steel is one of the few good trusts in this country.
TAFT TARGETS US STEEL
Angry that Taft was not carrying on his policies, Roosevelt decided to run in the 1912 presidential election.
I am as strong and fit as a bull moose. And that's my party now, the Progressive "Bull Moose" Party.
But the Bull Moose did not win this time. Instead, Democrat Woodrow Wilson was elected president.

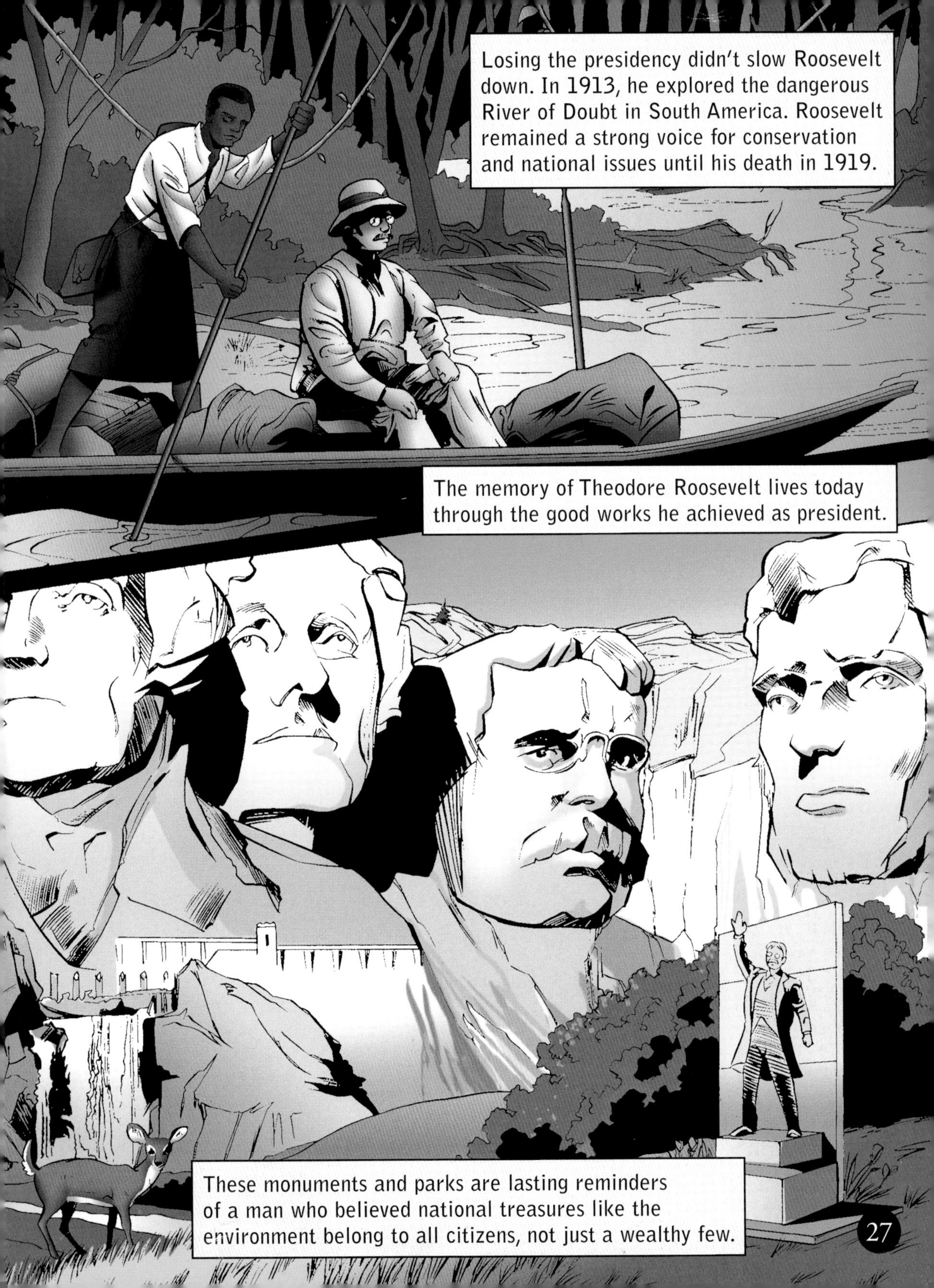
Losing the presidency didn't slow Roosevelt down. In 1913, he explored the dangerous River of Doubt in South America. Roosevelt remained a strong voice for conservation and national issues until his death in 1919.
The memory of Theodore Roosevelt lives today through the good works he achieved as president.
These monuments and parks are lasting reminders of a man who believed national treasures like the environment belong to all citizens, not just a wealthy few.

Theodore Roosevelt

 Theodore Roosevelt was born October 27, 1858, in New York City. He died January 6, 1919, at his home in Oyster Bay, New York, at age 60.

 In his youth, Roosevelt was known by the nickname Teedie. As an adult, he preferred the nickname TR. He never liked being called Teddy, but it is a nickname still used for him today.

 In November 1902, Roosevelt accepted an invitation to go bear hunting in Mississippi. To make sure the president got a bear, his hosts had a bear tied to a tree. Roosevelt refused to shoot the defenseless animal. Newspapers carried a political cartoon of the event and toy makers soon were selling toy bears called teddy's bear.

 Roosevelt had a way with words and was famous for his lively speeches. One of his most famous sayings was, "Speak softly and carry a big stick." Roosevelt meant that shouting threats was not the way to get your point across. It was enough if people knew you had the strength to back up your beliefs.

The home of the president in Washington, D.C., was officially known as the Executive Mansion. Most people called it the White House. When Roosevelt was president, he made the name change official. His stationery and press releases carried the official name White House. He thought this name was less stuffy than Executive Mansion.

 Theodore Roosevelt had six children. Alice was born just two days before her mother died. Roosevelt and his second wife, Edith, had five children, Theodore Jr., Kermit, Ethel, Archie, and Quentin.

 On October 14, 1912, Roosevelt was in Milwaukee, Wisconsin, walking from his hotel to the auditorium where he was scheduled to speak. A man suddenly came up, pulled a gun, and shot Roosevelt in the chest. The many sheets of folded paper holding Roosevelt's speech, plus his metal eyeglass case, slowed the bullet. Roosevelt was bleeding from the wound but insisted he make the speech. He began by saying, "I don't know whether you fully understand that I have just been shot, but it takes more than that to kill a Bull Moose."

Glossary

asthma (AZ-muh)—a condition that causes a person to wheeze and have difficulty breathing

canal (kuh-NAL)—a channel dug across land; canals connect bodies of water so that ships can travel between them.

corruption (kuh-RUHPT-shun)—the misuse of one's public job or office for personal gain

formaldehyde (for-MELD-uh-hide)—a chemical used as a preservative

influence (IN-floo-uhnss)—to have an effect on someone or something

specimen (SPESS-uh-muhn)—a sample that a scientist studies closely

trek (TREK)—a slow, difficult journey

trusts (TRUHSTZ)—businesses organized to stop competition so that the group makes more money

Internet Sites

FactHound offers a safe, fun way to find Internet sites related to this book. All of the sites on FactHound have been researched by our staff.

Here's how:
1. Visit *www.facthound.com*
2. Choose your grade level.
3. Type in this book ID **0736868496** for age-appropriate sites. You may also browse subjects by clicking on letters, or by clicking on pictures and words.
4. Click on the **Fetch It** button.

FactHound will fetch the best sites for you!

Read More

Anderson, Dale. *Building the Panama Canal.* Landmark Events in American History. Milwaukee: World Almanac, 2005.

Editors of Time For Kids with Lisa deMauro. *Theodore Roosevelt: The Adventurous President.* New York: HarperCollins, 2005.

Petersen, David. *National Parks.* A True Book. New York: Children's Press, 2001.

Santella, Andrew. *Roosevelt's Rough Riders.* We the People. Minneapolis: Compass Point Books, 2006.

Swain, Gwenyth. *Theodore Roosevelt.* History Maker Bios. Minneapolis: Lerner, 2005.

Bibliography

Brands, H. W. *T. R.: The Last Romantic.* New York: Basic Books, 1997

Morris, Edmund. *Theodore Rex.* New York: Random House, 2001.

Roosevelt, Theodore. *Theodore Roosevelt: An Autobiography.* New York: The MacMillian Company, 1913.

Roosevelt, Theodore. *The Rough Riders.* New York: G. P. Putnam's Sons, 1901.

Index